COMMUNITY, AS, AND COSMOS

---

*Toward a Phenomenological Interpretation
and Theology of Traditional
Afro-Christian Worship*

Gilbert I. Bond

University Press of America,® Inc.
Lanham · New York · Oxford

Copyright © 2002 by
University Press of America,® Inc.
4720 Boston Way
Lanham, Maryland 20706
UPA Acquisitions Department (301) 459-3366

12 Hid's Copse Rd.
Cumnor Hill, Oxford OX2 9JJ

Library of Congress Cataloging-in-Publication Data

Bond, Gilbert I.
Community, communitas, and cosmos : toward a
phenomenological interpretation and theology of traditional
Afro-Christian worship / Gilbert I. Bond.
p.   cm
Includes bibliographical references and index.
1. Salem Baptist Church (Atlanta, Ga.) 2. Baptists, Black—
Georgia—Atlanta—Religious life—Case studies. 3. Public
worship—Georgia—Atlanta—Case studies. 4. Public worship—
Baptists—Case studies. I. Title.

BX6480.A737 B66 2002
264'.06175818—dc21   2002028737 CIP

ISBN 0-7618-2377-8 (paperback : alk. ppr.)

Contents

iii

Preface

Many changes have taken place at Salem Baptist Church since I began this project in the last decade of the previous century. Salem has grown in membership, part of the "second northern invasion" of Atlanta. This time, however, the walls came tumblin' up, with the construction of an Eastside Sanctuary in Lithonia, and a registered membership of over 6,000. I have addressed the changes in Salem's liturgy in an article, "Psalms in a Contemporary African-American Church," included in *Biblical Texts in Community: The Psalms in Jewish and Christian Tradition: A Book of Essays and a DVD of Performance in Representative Styles with Commentary by Scholars, Performers, and Practitioners*, eds., Harold W. Attridge and Margot E. Fassler (publisher to be determined).

One dimension of Salem which remains unchanged are the traditional practices of African American Christian hospitality. I have been welcomed generously by every member of Salem's community upon every visit. Members of the Usher Board, Welcome Committee, Deacons, teachers, officer staff, communications staff, and many others were invaluable to this project. I cannot name everyone, but some require personal mention: Mother Morton, (the late) Deacon Napper, Phil Boyd, Mr. Mayfield, Reverend Joseph Williams, Revered Jasper Williams III, and Revered Jasper Williams, Jr., Pastor of Salem Missionary Baptist Church.

Anyone who has witnessed worship at Salem has been in the presence of a powerful nurturant community of faith, the core of African American Christianity at the height of its collective creativity. At the forefront of Salem's leadership is the liturgical genius of Reverend Jasper Williams, Jr., who Sunday after Sunday, in season and out, along with other members of the worship leadership, usher members into the invoked presence of the Spirit of the Living God who occupies the center of Salem's community, *communitas* and cosmos. To the leadership and the members of Salem Baptist Missionary Church I am and will forever remain grateful for their grace filled welcome of me and support of this project which is dedicated to them.

Finally, I must thank my Research Assistant, Ms. Angela McGraw whose patient, persistent and passionate commitment to the details of academic manuscript preparation, in season and out, proved to be more valuable than I could have imagined at the genesis of this work. For her faithfulness over things, few and many, words are not enough.

Gilbert I. Bond
Associate Professor of Theology
and African American Studies
The Divinity School
Yale University
New Haven, Connecticut

Chapter 1

Introduction

Overview

This project is a phenomenological study of three modes of collective religious interaction within a traditional urban Afro-Christian community of faith: the Wednesday night prayer meeting, the deacon's devotion, and the Sunday worship service as observed at Salem Baptist Church in Atlanta, Georgia. The three modes are similar in that each shapes the interactions and utterances of the participants, in relation to one another and to God. Yet each mode is characterized by distinctive elements and teleology. Understood as formalistic, repetitive patterns of behavior, the three settings qualify as ritual.[1] As patterned activity which seeks and waits upon sacred power, the settings incline toward liturgy.[2] The liturgical characterization, however, immediately poses methodological difficulties. Liturgy as traditionally studied focuses primarily upon written texts which exist both apart from and within the moment of ritual praxis. Yet the community of faith at Salem Baptist Church belongs to a tradition devoted to hearing the Biblical word and memorizing its extensive corpus. Salem emphasizes the oral and extemporaneous rather than the written address to God.

These three terrains of religious activity provide an opportunity to develop an interpretation that moves beyond the conventional understanding of ritual and liturgy toward a phenomenological investigation of religious experience within a traditional Black church. My approach entails a careful description of the three realms in order to present as fully as possible the multiple dimensions of the participants' experience. Spiegelberg's term for such an approach is "descriptive phenomenology."[3] I have combined the descriptive with the interpretive in order to offer a cultural hermeneutic phenomenology which discloses aspects of New World African culture and experience that are historically embedded within religious ritual.   The horizon toward which this study opens can be identified as a movement from phenomenological empiricism to questions of philosophical phenomenology or "second phenomenology."[4] This methodological trajectory may provide the point of entry for theological reflection on and interpretation of contemporary Black Christianity: a phenomenologically-based theology of Black people's experience of affliction, community, and transformative suffering in God.

Congregational Portrait

With an average attendance of 1,400 to 1,500 weekly, and an enrolled membership of over 2,000, Salem Baptist Church of Atlanta occupies an undeniably important role in the lives of its members. Attendance and membership figures alone, however, do not begin to access the significance of this church. Through the use and mastery of modern communications technology, Salem has broadened its influence throughout Atlanta, Georgia and into households throughout the nation. In Atlanta, Salem's services are seen in more than 14,000 homes on Sunday evening, making it the most popular program on channel 69. With cable network, Salem enters major urban markets throughout the north and south.

The success of Salem's appeal can be attributed in large but not exclusive measure to the power and *charism* of Pastor Jasper Williams. His mastery of a traditional style of Afro-Christian preaching, known as "whooping," as well as his thoroughly researched, well-prepared and clearly presented Scripture lessons makes him an attractive figure for several media and the growing popularity of the "electronic church" within the Black communities of the African Diaspora.[5]   To understand the appeal and power of the Wednesday evening prayer meeting, however, we must temporarily ignore the undeniable gravity of Pastor Williams and turn to a closer examination of the events and participants that make up the occasion.

Walter Pitt describes the Afro-Baptist church as a "working-class" phenomenon, distinct from both the Primitive Baptist (lower economic fundamentalist) and the "middle-class Black Baptist."[6] While these socio-economic categories may accurately describe churches in rural areas, Pitt's distinction loses applicability in Atlanta and other urban settings, where churches are developing a far more heterogeneous profile. Middle-class congregants are highly visible and numerous across several generations at Salem, along with working-class and marginally employed members. The pastor as well as his parishioners are extremely proud of his degree from Morehouse University; the diploma occupies a prominent position in the display case located in the narthex. Pastor William's pedagogical and homiletical style are further indicators of a church well-integrated across previously exclusive social boundaries. While his Scriptural lessons include knowledge gathered beyond the confines of the Black religious folk tradition, his sermons derive their power by remaining within traditional aesthetic and stylistic boundaries. He is therefore capable of addressing a pluralistic audience with various levels of literacy and divergent backgrounds within a single worship service.

We therefore cannot approach the study of Salem's rituals from a singular socio-economic perspective or a singular tradition. Historical sociological analysis is helpful in locating Salem's relationship to other churches and its place within an established tradition, but is of limited service in assisting our understanding of the existential experience and event of prayer. If Salem owes part of its unique identity to the development of a pluralistic community, the crucial question is not whether this development represents historical continuity or discontinuity. Rather the target of inquiry is what provides the basis of a commonality that is capable of appealing to and satisfying the complex needs of a diverse population.

The general answer is that Salem utilizes traditional Black church resources to address the diversified needs of its membership for the purpose of creating a unique community. Melvin D. Williams, in the context of studying a Black Pentecostal church, defined community as "patterned interactions among a delineated group of individuals who seek security, support, identity, and significance from their group..."[7] Phenomenology offers an additional dimension to Williams' definition by describing a process of inter-subjective experience of mutually disclosed internality, that is, an experience that enables participants to empathically enter each other's interiority. We will now examine formation of community through one of the consistently reliable means of fostering relationships within the church: the weekly prayer meeting.

Chapter 2

Two Wednesday Night Prayer Meetings

Context

Prayer meetings, which include Bible study, are regularly scheduled every Wednesday evening from 7:00 to 8:00 p.m. The Wednesday night prayer meeting is the gathering attended by every member with serious commitment and heartfelt need. Traditionally, Wednesday night occupied a pivotal position in the arduous life of working Black people. For the millions of Black women employed as "domestics," a term used to describe those who made a living cooking, cleaning, and caring for the families and homes of relatively affluent white people, Thursday was the one day they could expect to take off. Weekends and weekdays would find them in kitchens away from home. These women could therefore afford to extend Wednesday night into the late hours of intensive and shared prayer. The importance of this service has become so widespread and central in the lives of believers that it has entered into the collective imagination of the Black community, providing creative material for musicians, artists and writers.[1] Smaller churches could expect to find the majority of its members present. At Salem, however, the percentage is much smaller, but not less crucial to the life of the church and the success of the Sunday worship.

The majority of attendants are women. This percentage is consistent with figures found throughout an institution whose membership is 75% female.[2] Women are proportionally over- represented among the laity, while under-represented within the hierarchy. The visible hierarchy consists almost exclusively of male leadership. Women exercise and wield far greater power, however, than their absence from formal roles of leadership suggests. Since the focus of this monograph does not include the social-political dimensions of communal relationships, the role and place of gender beyond the confines of ritual are not discussed. Instead the focus will be upon the performance of the ritual and its multiple implications for the life of the believer. Overall attendance vacillates between 80 to 200 participants depending upon the number and nature of competing guild, staff, and board meetings held during the same hour. Men are always present at the prayer meeting, composing 20-25% of the gathering on any given occasion during my visits.

The most notable element within these meetings is that the absence of the pastor, Pastor Williams, is yet permeated by his presence. Given Salem's burgeoning mission and membership, some time ago the church reached the point where multiple staff was absolutely necessary. Even beyond the obviously impossible task of attending every one of his church's activities, Pastor Williams, unlike his rural or small urban church counterpart, is not one to be casually encountered. Neither his style nor role allow him to be seen in the midst of the Friday night fish fry or the sand-lot baseball game. His members usually wait until Sunday to see their head pastor on a very limited basis. Yet, despite the degree to which he is absent, his presence is strongly felt. The first object to arrest the eye in the fellowship hall is the huge studio photograph of Pastor Williams hung on the wall across from the entrance. Immediately next to his portrait is one of Pastor Williams' predecessor, Pastor Jackson. Together the two images represent continuity from one generation to the next. The history represented in these figures is very important to a church that is 98 years old. Beyond their cognitive dimension, however, these portraits function in a religious-iconographic manner to communicate the presence of one who is acknowledged as being close to an extraordinary power of the divine, and who is capable of providing to members access to its domain.

Congregants and visitors do not attend the prayer service expecting to encounter Pastor Williams. Leadership is provided by Assistant Reverend Sypho, a young man who dresses in the garb of ecclesiastical importance: colorful pants of contemporary styling, coats with a modern cut, bright ties, pastel shirts. Rev. Sypho's presentations are powerful, yet his presence facilitates rather than dominates the occasions, in contrast to the commanding style of Pastor Williams.

Prayer Meeting I

Thirty minutes before the prayer meeting begins, the large fellowship hall is empty. The warm tone of the carpet softens the rough impact of concrete walls and steel girders and reinforcements of the high ceiling. Unlike the sanctuary, the fellowship hall serves multiple functions. Absent are crimson and purple tapestry, crucifix, stained glass, and pulpit furniture. In place of fixed pews are purple upholstered movable chairs arranged in three sections to form a semi-circle. Inside their arc a microphone sits in front of a nondescript table upon which rest the offering plates. Immediately behind the table is an elevated platform with a simple wooden podium and microphone. There are four seats where Rev. Sypho sits on occasion, or a guest speaker. Another level rises behind with an additional row of seats, which remain unoccupied and serve to keep the first-level occupants in the foreground. On either side of the platform are large stands of colorful artificial flowers. Together they frame the semblance of a pulpit and create an area on which to focus. Other than these suggestions of familiar furnishings, the space is open to the structuring of a variety of occasions by participants.

Women enter in clusters of two and three, neatly dressed, hair styled, wearing earrings and touches of make-up. Some are wearing office attire, while others have dressed specifically for the occasion. Another group has come straight from home and appear slightly worn in comparison to the Sunday-perfect appearance of their sisters. A few have children in tow and sit immediately to calm their rambunctious energy before the meeting begins. Others cross the room to exchange warm greetings and engage in a few minutes of fellowship. Those who enter alone tend to sit alone and read their Bibles. The men always sit in the last few rows, except for the clergy who take their seats in the front row or mount the platform. These cells of fellowship almost always remain neatly grouped by gender.

Those who regularly attend the evening prayer services, in season and out, are not only given to prayer, but to each other. They are people who are often burdened by the travails of others as well as their own, for they are led to regular participation in these meetings out of faith and suffering. Regular participants are often known as "prayer warriors" of the church. Members who do not attend these evening vigils can call upon the "warriors" for prayerful support. They can be entrusted with the painful and otherwise embarrassing needs of a family in trouble, conflicted spouses, errant children. Others perceive the "warriors" as possessing a more reliable access to God: "I got a telephone in my heart, and I can call Him up any time" (Sister Rosetta Thorpe).

From amidst this group arise "the saints," the term designating the unofficial election of those known for the depth of their witness to God. It is important to disentangle this term from its conventional connotations which, in America, suggest a person of outstanding moral virtues. Even popular Christian wisdom on this subject fails to adequately capture the resonances of its use within Black church communities. The title, most often used in the collective, refers less to moral exemplars who are noted for outstanding Christian achievements than to those with a special depth of relationship with Jesus, and response to suffering. "Saints" are those who live by faith and prayer, and in so doing have grown larger than the pain which besets their life. For all their joy, they have endured an undeniable element of tragedy in their lives. The "saints" are therefore regarded with a respect which borders upon homage, for above any other measure, the tragic marks which cut across the face of their faith identify their proximity to the presence of Jesus. Other members are drawn to these prayer meetings out of occasional crisis, or have become regular attendants after a transforming experience. Some simply enjoy the interaction with others. The reasons are various, but the results are similar: the creation of a community of intense fellowship within the vastly larger population of Salem Baptist.

Both the space of the room and the structure of the meeting invite a more loosely interactive form of participation than the Sunday morning worship. Unlike the sanctuary, the fellowship hall does not have a sacred center of gravity that pulls one toward it and commands a reflexive reverential attitude, posture and speech when entering its presence. More than any other devotional occasion, the prayer meeting depends upon the shared creation of sacred space, a transformation of neutral terrain to a sacred frame of reference. Unassisted by sacred objects, which demarcate this realm, the responsibility becomes a shared effort on the part of those present.

Even though the prayer meeting does not proceed according to a strict rite, events do follow an established pattern of repeated action and utterance designed to create and fulfill a socially intended effect; i.e., the prayer meeting is a ritual. Of primary importance, and first in order of events, is the task of gathering the disparate and segregated clusters of fellowship into a unified body. After a last minute sound check by a technician, preparations are complete. The service commences with the arrival of the first speaker to the microphone. While each meeting is initiated by an announcement by one standing upon the platform, a large number of members are eligible to execute this function. On three different occasions, three different members fulfilled this responsibility: two lay persons and Rev. Sypho. Lay persons are often members of one of the church's numerous guilds or committees, or are simply individual members. They need not bring prior authority or ordination in order to be effective. When Rev. Sypho is not presiding, he nonetheless remains seated on the first elevated row of the platform behind the presider *pro tempore.*

Rev. Sypho stands, opens his Bible, and begins: "Giving honor, thanks and praise unto Almighty God..." This invocational form precedes every other statement and event in every prayer service. The phrase sounds formulaic, yet never loses its power to bring an event into a devotional state. Throughout the prayer meeting, these words will be repeated often, as, for example, when members from the floor approach the microphone to give testimony or to introduce themselves or another member, guest or visitor in the body. The phrase serves to re-position the speaker by displacing him or her personally from the center of significance and heightening the congregation's focus upon the actions taking place before them. These sparse words which flow effortlessly from every member who utters them are theologically laden with inflected descriptions of the divine. They signal, whenever they are uttered, a reminder of the appropriate disposition one needs to assume before God. I will return to this theme later. For now, it is important to identify this motif as one which will be repeated throughout the evening.

Rev. Sypho reads from Genesis 3:15, the divinely promised antagonism between the woman and the serpent. The theme for this month is "Satan." The thematic element is one mark of Salem's modernity and a departure from the more traditional prayer meetings, which allowed each occasion to define its own focus. Sustained thematic approaches to sermons, Scripture study, and worship have developed throughout Protestant churches in America. Many denominations follow the lectionary as one example of introducing new liturgical organization into more Evangelical churches. This is not to suggest that Protestant worship, Black or white, has been without form or regularity. On the contrary, Black churches have time-honored and unbroken habits and forms shaped and sustained by the power of ritual. What is new can be found in the influence of an increasingly educated clergy and laity, who introduces and expects forms of organization that reflect a more self-conscious approach to church. The thematic element indicates the influence of systematic approaches to activity and thought usually found within the world of business, marketing and media. While these elements permeate America's dominant white and managerial culture, Black culture continues to be characterized by ritual interaction rather than by systematic management. Thematic approaches to Scripture study

within the context of ritual thus point to the strength and flexibility of
the Black church in assimilating technocratic elements from beyond its
cultural boundaries and in adapting them to ritualistic ends.

After reading, Rev. Sypho asks us to stand, turn to our brother or
sister, extend our hand and say, "I love you; God loves you: You have
a savior in Jesus!" The shift in focus seems abrupt and forced, but the
words and actions begin to erode, ever so awkwardly, the walls of
distance and personal isolation. By the time we have repeated these
words and gestures to several people in our vicinity, they begin to feel
natural. In the midst of our greetings, Rev. Sypho invites Deacon
Christy forward to lead us in song. An elderly man with a leonine
shock of white hair comes forward with a Bible, turns toward the
congregation, and without microphone belts out the first line:

> I got a home, waiting for me...waiting for me, waiting for me, I got
> a home, waiting for me...

Deacon Christy sways, taps his feet, and slaps his Bible in time, his
body becoming the rhythm of the congregation, who begin to sway in
unison, returning his gestures and accents. Deacon Christy leads us
through several verses of this hymn which, while rhythmic,
nevertheless retain a mournful tone characteristic of selections made by
deacons of his generation. The elders' musical orientation is "pre-
gospel" music, reaching back into a rural musical form which
developed prior to the advent of the more popular urban high-energy
music identified with the contemporary Black church.

Rev. Sypho, who has been standing on the platform, swaying and
intoning behind Deacon Christy, steps toward the microphone as the
hymn concludes. He signals the congregation to be seated, calls forth
the members of the Usher Board, and indicates that they will assume
leadership for tonight's meeting. In four simple actions: 1) reading
from Scripture, 2) standing, 3) greeting, 4) shared singing of a hymn,
those present have moved from discrete clusters and isolated
individuals to a connected and focused body. When they take their
seats again, they are not the same people who entered fifteen minutes
ago; they are a tentative collective moving toward greater connection
with each other.

The four actions are repeated in some variation at every prayer
meeting at Salem. Together these actions compose the transitional
phase of the ritual which accomplishes three essential tasks: 1) moving
people across the boundary from the workday world into the prayer
meeting; 2) dissolving the isolated singularity of identity and role,
with allegiances to more limited and enclosed social cells, into a
shared identity; and finally, 3) creating and demarcating a devotional

space for and of the sacred. Six women walk forward, Bibles in hand, forming a rank; they turn and face the congregation. Each in turn reads Genesis 3:15, 1 Peter 5:8, Ephesians 5:26-7, I Thessalonians 2:4, I Thessalonians 3:5, and John 12:38.

The Scriptures follow the theme of struggle with the demonic. The tableau of Scripture readers turns the members' attention not outward upon those who stand before them, but inward. After the introductory period of intense interaction, now the members enter into a more reflective mode as the Biblical passages are slowly read by the members of the Usher Board. At first glance, this turn toward the interior seems to oppose the direction of the first section of the ritual, which created an experience focussed upon the group rather than the individual. Yet the shared sense of mutual identity generated through interaction does not disintegrate during the moments of personal reflection. Most of those present have personal Bibles customized for Salem Baptist Church. The pagination and style are uniform. When the verses are announced, the page numbers are included. The contemplative act of Scripture reading and meditation is actually more cenobitic than atomistic, retaining the character of the group's shared activity achieved in the first section of the evening's ritual. The presiding member of the Usher Board invites everyone to stand and recite the Lord's Prayer. People then reach out and take one another's hand and begin in unison. The rhythmic recitation of these familiar verses pulls the focus outward: in gesture toward one's neighbor; in address, toward God. The ritual has come full circle, returning to the theme embedded in Rev. Sypho's opening acknowledgement, "Giving all honor, thanks and praise unto almighty God, the Father," and to the interpersonal dimensions which build the necessary community for prayer. Both aspects come together powerfully in this ritualistic recitation. In one sense, the prayer meeting begins with this prayer, for the members have begun to pray to God as a community.

The second main division in this evening's prayer meeting is indicated by a shift in focus. When the meeting moves in a different direction, it does not always assume the same form. Rev. Sypho may preach, or a guest minister may present a Bible study followed by a sermon, or on still other occasions, members from the floor may provide a solo rendition of a heartfelt hymn or gospel song. This section can also be structured by the personal testimonies of the laity, in verbal or musical form. The unique role in the ritual, which the middle section occupies, is distinguished not by its specific content but rather by the open space and flexible opportunity to be shaped according to the designs and spontaneous needs of the members.

As the members return to their seats, a man approaches the microphone. He is in his late twenties, very casually dressed in a short-sleeved knit pullover shirt, and a toothpick in his hair above his right ear. He is a member of the Usher Board and a lay person. He reads from Isaiah 14: 12-20, concerning the fate of Lucifer, and begins his presentation. (The congregation's response here and elsewhere is noted in brackets.)

You know God works in mysterious ways. [Amen, that's right] But the Devil works in mysterious ways as well. [Yesss...] We have to remember that in Ephesians, God tells us to keep on the full armor of God (Ephesians 6:11). [Teach now, teach] You see, the Devil goes to church! [That's right, now] You can see the Devil in a nice dress, hair all made up, pretty earrings, purse, and make-up. Wearing a big smile and speaking sweet. [Oh yes, Lord; talk about it] But the Devil also comes dressed in a three-piece suit! [Well] Smelling good, with gold around the neck, pretty shoes, bright shirt, button-down. Driving a fine ride! [Tell the truth] So tonight, we just want to "pause for the cause" and give God the glory, because God saw something in you that nobody else saw. [Yes sir] As Pastor Williams has said to us so many times: "God is the reason for the season." [Yes He is] You see, people, we have got it all backwards. I saw somebody the other day while I was driving with a bumper sticker that said, "God is my co-pilot." [Well] Brothers and Sisters, God does not need you for a pilot, and you do not need God for a co-pilot... [Come on now, that's right] We need God for a pilot, not no co-pilot! [applause, shouts, amens]

The young man's sermonette has introduced a new energy into the meeting and shifted the lines of interaction from within the group to the exchange between the members and the person standing before them. The interactive valence between individual and community characterizes the mid-section of each prayer meeting. Two very important aspects of his presentation are to be noted. One is the style of his language. This aspect of the evening's ritual draws heavily upon another ritual with which Black Americans who have grown up within the culture of the traditional community are thoroughly familiar: "signifying." Signifying (in its more aggressive form) is a ritual of oblique verbal insults. The ritual takes place within a social setting and draws its power from the skill with which the speaker devalues his target in a manner that does not name the person, but identifies him or her in a way that is immediately recognizable to the audience. Signification always contains an element of humor, even when the intent is hostile. On this occasion the speaker is signifying–generally considered a profane instrument of personal derogation and social discord–for the purpose of exposing an unnamed activity that destroys the unity of the church. In so doing, he creates a consensus among the members through his indirect reference, characteristic of all forms of signifying, to the practice of coming to church with the intent of attracting the attention of the opposite sex. Within the context of religious ritual he has transformed a profane act into a sacred act, thus creating what signification ordinarily can never achieve: social unity and harmony. In the act of signifying on those who attend church with duplicitous intentions, he has expressed another dimension of collective identity. One begins to gain a sense of the multi-textured meanings which each act and word assumes in Black religious ritual.

The first speaker is followed by a young woman in a floral dress who mounts the platform. She opens her Bible and pauses. Rev. Sypho looks on from his seat on the platform, while the members focus upon her. She begins with the honorary acknowledgement: "First, giving honor to Our Lord and Savior, and my Brothers and Sisters in Christ." She repeats the theme for the month, "Satan," but adds to this Biblical designation of the term "Devil" the Black community's terms of derogation: "signifier" and "liar." One could view the use of these terms as communal-cultural exegesis of the Biblical text. By naming the Devil a "signifier" and a "liar," she is interpreting the text from the perspective of the Black church tradition and its familiarity with the social dynamics of those who remain outside the church. A well-known gospel song contains the verse,

> Satan is a liar and a conjurer too,
> If you don't watch out
> he'll conjure you [3]

A very rich dialogue is in progress, defining the important opposition between what Black believers call "the world" and "living in Jesus." One ritual practice is confronting another.

"How can we defeat Satan?" the woman asks the church. She then begins a narrative which recounts the arrival of Satan upon earth. Her narrative draws heavily upon Christian mythology of Lucifer which is only suggested in Scripture (cf. Isaiah 14:12-20; Luke 10:18), but which developed more imaginative elaborations over the centuries. Without opening a discussion of comparative demonology, I simply want to point here to one dimension among others that is singularly Afro-American. In the eyes of the Black church, Satan retains a comical element to his behavior and personality. In part this is due to the degree to which he is depicted as a trickster figure whose impish instigations are humorously retold in folk tales and toasts. Within the context of the evening's ritual, however, this part of his identity is used as a form of ritualized denigration. For example, after reciting the tale of Lucifer's fall, the speaker reads Genesis 3: 3-5. The serpent's actions not only disrupt the relationship of the man and woman, but result in the serpent's demise. "Satan, that ol' fool!" she says repeatedly with emphasis. She is practicing a form of mockery and humiliation found in rituals of healing and exorcism among primal peoples. In contrast to the preceding speaker, who spoke of Satan figuratively as a style of deceit and discord among members of the church, the woman is dissociating Satan from any personal incarnation through her use of mythological narrative and ritual devaluation.

This point is of crucial importance not only in describing the purposes and functions of the evening's ritual, but also in defining the nature of theological discourse within the Black church. Theological language in this tradition takes place within a ritual setting wherein denotative, connotative, typological, figurative and literal modes of utterance operate *simultaneously*. This point is essential to an understanding of the distinction between the Evangelical heritage within which the Black church emerged, and the highly figurative and symbolic uses of language which inform and express Black religious traditions. These uses are shaped both by an African *poesis* and by a history of oppressive relationships with people who define and legitimate the "acceptable" language of religious experience. The language of faith among Black people is poetic by necessity and heritage.

The woman continues with her exegesis. From the behavior of the serpent, she turns her attention to that of the woman and man. "They yielded to the temptation of the Devil!" Another woman stands and begins an *a cappella* rendition of "Yield Not To Temptation." The meeting is assuming form and pattern. One could expect an appropriately selected piece of music to echo the speaker's key phrases. The musical addition, however, is not simply a matter of "slick programming." Music, especially when performed by a soloist, demands serious attention, conveys tremendous power, and evokes profound emotions. The singer's voice is heavy and strains toward the rising notes. Her efforts create a stage upon which dramatic impressions of spiritual struggle are enacted. Biblical interpretation from this perspec-tive is not a cerebral affair, but has more in common with the roots of ancient theater wherein religion, ritual, and drama were one. The Black church maintains the organic relationship between these now disparate forms, traditions unraveled in the West by tradition and time.

He will carry you through...

Her final verse sung, the singer returns to her seat.   The speaker picks up this verse and uses it as a transition to the next Biblical passage:

He will carry you through...if you trust Him

She reads from Mark 4: 14-15: Jesus' parable of the sower of the good word stolen by Satan. She interpolates, beginning with the "word," which she understands as the Gospel, the good news. She then moves to the "good word," spoken by Jesus. The "good word" is the "good news" of salvation which is the source of our joy. "Satan will steal your joy," she warns the members. "We should depend upon God's Amazing Grace."   Another woman stands and sings in slow, chant style this enduring jewel of Black hymnology.[4]   "Amazing Grace" together with Tom Dorsey's "Precious Lord" compose the crown of Black devotional music.   The congregation joins the singer in this almost mournful rendition.

Although the musical selections are performed by different soloists, each singer shapes and sustains the emotional tenor of the service established by the speaker's earlier intonations.   Black performance styles are capable of creating subtle differentiations of feeling within a larger emotional spectrum.   The combination of rhythmic variations and individual stylistic improvisations is a source of endless re-workings of familiar material that can respond to the vicissitudes of religious experience.

[The speaker continues]: Let's go to Revelation 12:9. "And the great dragon was cast out, that old serpent, called the Devil, and Satan, which deceiveth the whole world: he was cast out into the earth, and his angels were cast out with him." God has angels, but the Devil has angels! [Oh yes, that's right]   What can we do? One, thank God. Two, pray to be filled with the Holy Spirit. Three, put on the whole armor. [Yes Lord, yes] If you put on the whole armor, then Satan's angels cannot come against you! You must stand and you will prevail, for God is not through blessing you.

Another soloist rises and sings along with the speaker's last line. The integration of Bible readings, commentary and song flows effortlessly at this part of the service, creating a seamless fabric of dramatic interpretation, instruction and exhortation. The melding of spoken and sung word in public exegesis of the text, which depicts the moral struggle as a spiritual struggle, turns the prayer meeting into a single, highly elaborate topology.   Watching and hearing the service develop in all of its elaborate unfolding is like witnessing a multi-hued cathedral rose window slowly assume form before one's eyes.

James 4:7 is the final reading. The selection is carefully chosen, for it brings the sung and spoken impressionistic portraits to a dramatic, yet somewhat humorous, conclusion.

Submit yourselves therefore to God. Resist the devil, and he will flee from you. Submit yourself–who to, Satan? No, to God! [Hands are raised in the gesture, which affirms the truth of what is spoken, but also signals the presence of the Holy Spirit] [Yes, yes] The Devil is a coward!! [Oh yes] But we are going to march against sin and the Devil.

A woman begins to sing, "Satan, We Going to Tear Your Kingdom Down." The members are on their feet, rocking, singing and clapping in time. The song is highly spirited, yet retains its tone of serious intent. The struggle against Satan has turned into a rout. At the song's conclusion, while we are still standing, Rev. Sypho resumes leadership, marking the start of the ritual's third and concluding section. He invites three women and four men to lift up in prayer the needs and special requests which have been made by the members and by others who are not present. As those who will pray come forth, the mood subtly shifts as the members slow their pace from the energetic triumphalism to a more somber reverence. Prayers for individuals, groups and the more inclusive concerns of the church and community are named. "With every head bowed, every eye closed..." Rev. Sypho implores. The first woman prays:

Almighty God and Father, we come before You tonight with a humble heart asking that You look down upon us with mercy. We pray for Mrs. _____, Lord, that You would touch her body and remove the affliction from her. Father, and for all those who suffer, in body and mind, we ask that You would send healing, Lord, this evening. We need You Lord, we need You right now, we pray, ha'mercy.

Many prayers follow this pattern of pleading and supplication in a spontaneous and informal, yet passionate manner. The phrases are not as formulaic as those one would hear during the Sunday morning devotion or the worship service. More of a rawness emerges in the members' prayers, an unhewn quality which follows the shape of immediate and personal need. The cadence is less predictable than in other prayer forms, but it is precisely this unpredictable, spontaneous quality which marks the uniqueness of the Wednesday night prayer meeting at Salem.

Rev. Sypho's prayers, by contrast, follow a more familiar pattern of rising intensity and rhythmic, rhetorical style. For example:

> We bow our heads, God, to say thank You. We thank You today, God, for the ministry You have given this church, We thank You for the shepherd You have planted in this vineyard.   We always will continue to give Thy name and to praise Thy name the glory.   And as simple as it may seem, I want to take time to thank You, Father, for the wisdom and the knowledge [Yes sir] with which You have crowned Pastor Williams' head and the vision that You have given him. I thank You, eternal God, for lifting him up when he's down, I thank You for giving him a zeal to pour out Your word to thy people. We as a church family tonight just come before You, just praising Your name, saying Lord, we really do thank You. Then, our Father, as we bow tonight, we realize that all is not well...some people are less fortunate than those who are in this building. There are those who have drug problems, and, God, cannot seem to find the answer to their problems, we are praying tonight that You will let them know that You are God, that You still hold all power in Your hands.

Rev. Sypho's prayers are structured with a musical pulse that carries his phrases. He is not the only one who is capable of presenting public prayer in this manner. Salem has its share of "prayer warriors" who can move others to tears with their soulful and structured utterances. But there are many more people who are drawn to the evening meetings out of need and who pray in a less artful but no less authentic fashion.

Within the prayer service, one can see the church in its constituent and varied elements perhaps more clearly than in any other communal activity. Prayer meetings are a people's church, a form of worship from the bottom up. The more formal rites which shape and structure the Sunday worship and which depend upon highly specialized functions executed by officers, artists, and technicians of the sacred are absent. In their place are laity who bring a variety of needs and skills and who shape the worship within a more basic framework. The church hierarchy of members who embody and generate energy and power within the Sunday worship is represented by Rev. Sypho. Yet he does not dominate these proceedings. Rather, his presence represents the official leadership of the church, and his role is to facilitate the order of the service.

While the Sunday devotional and worship services provide ample room for participation, their direction and character lead to a culminating focus on the hierarchy, particularly the pastor. Sunday's service, however, does not provide the space and opportunity for public forms of intimacy which pull members into the each other's lives. Here the focus is more diffuse and changing, moving from person to person, as each makes an individual contribution to the evening's service. Prayer meetings always have an unpredictable edge to them. One can never quite anticipate the manner in which they will unfold. Each week, therefore, is a distinctive service. Yet the monthly theme provides continuity in the midst of ongoing variations.

The events described above amply illustrate the firm hand which the hierarchy holds upon the shape of the service. The most severe imposition is the one-hour limit upon the meeting. In response to my inquiries, members revealed that the prayer meeting was not always dominated by ministerial leaders. For years, members met in each other's homes for prayer, testifying, music and meals on Wednesday nights. These house meetings were organized and led by lay leaders, and provided an egalitarian shape to the services. These meetings, with unstructured space and open-ended time, had the flexibility to expand or contract according to the felt needs of the participants. Many of the meetings would be sponsored by women. This information suggests the need for a more in-depth study of the role of female leadership in the church outside the visibly male-dominated hierarchy. Correlations between the type of activity, style of leader-ship, and shape of events might be directly related to gender-specific influences. For now, it should be noted that the earlier style of open-ended prayer meetings–a far cry from Salem's current well-coordinated management of time and theme (a sign of urban modernity)–was an indispensable element in the creation of liminal space and time, always necessary for the creation and emergence of a bonded community.[5]

The prayer meeting at Salem displays traces of its amalgamated heritage. On the one hand, there is the presence of ordained (male) officers of the church; hierarchical control of the service's theme; appropriation of the meeting for emphasizing and reinforcing goals of ministerial leadership; and minimal time provided for the prayers of laity. As an alternating layer, the traditions and influence of the laity are manifest in the prevalence of testimony and the spontaneous, improvised modes of prayer and song.

I include below a description of another Wednesday night prayer service since this particular meeting embodies elements of both the church-hierarchy and laity-led service.

Prayer Meeting II

This prayer meeting occurred during an extensive church-wide campaign to build a retirement home on land adjacent to Salem

Baptist. Despite months of planning and prayerful deliberation, the project was languishing in the face of reluctance by the landowners to relinquish the land necessary to the project's completion. This prayer meeting displays both the leadership in worship and the personal testimony of a single layperson, Linda Perkins, who moves between the two roles in the service. The description begins with the formal presentation by Linda, which will be followed by her testimony:

> Good evening to everyone: to Pastor Williams in his absence, to Rev. Sypho, to the Sons of Salem, and to my church family. I'm happy to be here this evening, for truly I know that God is able. [Amen] And I'm a living witness that I can stretch my hand to Him, and that He will answer–and He has answered, and He continues to answer my prayers.
>
> Last month we talked about...our theme was "Satan." And in meditating last week, the Lord put it upon my heart, and I called Rev. Sypho and I said, "I'll have a word to share if you don't mind, and at some time would you please let me share this Word." God has given me something, and when God gives it to you, its better to obey and to do what He has told you to do.
>
> Thinking about the month of stewardship, I didn't realize it at the time and it really didn't hit me until today what the Lord had given me. And so I want to share it with you, and I have called this topic: "Concerning This House." And if you have your Bibles, turn to I Kings 6:12-14. And it reads:
>
> "Concerning this house which thou art building, if thou wilt walk in my statutes, and execute my judgements, and keep all my commandments to walk in them; then will I perform my word with thee, which I spake unto David thy father...And I will dwell among the children of Israel, and will not forsake my people Israel. So Solomon built the house, and finished it."
>
> I wanted to share a word with you this evening concerning this house. More particularly, I wanted to have a word with King Solomon. I wanted to share a moment of conversation with a King who is experienced in this business of building a temple for the Lord. So if you don't mind tonight, bear with me and share with me, please, because I thought that it might be helpful, it might be a helpful exchange of ideas if we looked to Solomon and talked with Solomon tonight.
>
> I really thought that it might be to our advantage to review the matter of building a building with a King who has already lifted up from the ground an edifice for the King of Kings. I just wanted to have a word

with King Solomon. I need for you to bear with me, there's no light up here so it is a little difficult to see, so if I stumble along, just pray with me [That's alright] and the Lord will make it alright. [Well]

At this point we should note that Linda has approached the text of the Bible by first invoking the very characters who will appear in the narrative. By declaring her intention to seek the counsel of Solomon as a conversational partner concerning the plans to erect a home for the elderly, she has in effect established Solomon as a member of the community before referring to him as a character in the text.

Solomon, you will recall, reigned over the kingdom of Israel from 931 to 910 B.C. Solomon was the second son of David and Bathsheba. He knew what it was to sit on a pinnacle of renown, and he was reared as a royal prince. He came to power in the tenderness of youth. Nathan, the prophet, saw in Solomon the symbol of eternal forgiveness. And so he gave him an additional name, Jediah, for he was "the beloved of God." And you will recall that Solomon was known for his wisdom. It was said that Solomon was the composer of 3,000 proverbs, as well as 1,000 songs. Solomon was skilled in matters of governmental and military administration and in the arena of international diplomacy. Solomon knew no peer. But that's not why I wanted to have a dialogue with Solomon. I wanted to look to Solomon tonight because I thought *we* might do well, and I might do well, to have an understanding of Solomon's wisdom.

Solomon made his way to Gideon and there in a dream, God asked Solomon what he would want. And Solomon said, "I want an understanding mind. Give, therefore, Thy servant an understanding heart to judge Thy people, that I may discern between good and evil." And so perhaps I ought to say that you cannot build the house of God unless you have an understanding heart. And I declare that with it, you will become acquainted with good and evil. Solomon could have easily passed on the building plans to someone else. And that's why I wanted to talk with him, too, because I know he didn't have an easy time...

The members turn to the passage in I Kings and read in silence the text which is recited from the lectern. It is important to distinguish between the book as object and what is known in this setting as "the Word." This designation always refers to an articulated, announced utterance of God. The "Word" is an implied verb: active, vital, dynamic, but rarely used as an equivalent to the "Book," which occupies a place of significance and sanctity in other religious communities. The status of the "Word" is not that of liturgical object or a site of divine presence to be objectively uplifted. Traditional Black churches understand not the text, but its content (referent) as holy. The text itself is functional, not sacramental. It does not participate or share in the dimensions of the sacred to which it refers. Here the text/object serves as a portable sign or emblem of membership in the Salem community, an expression of commitment to the body and a deepening of one's devotional life. Possessing the Bible is not mandatory. The word achieves power through oral articulation, not visual interpretation. Those without a Bible before them become attuned and oriented toward the speaker as she invokes the dynastic ruler of Israel. The invocation does not depend upon rite. In fact, the attitude of Linda and her fellow congregants is more accurately described as acknowledgement rather than invocation, for she assumes that Solomon is already a participating presence, a relational presence. He is, therefore, addressed as a member of the body of believers, an ancestor who can be called upon for guidance, wisdom, and counsel in the hour of the community's need.

History in this realm is not linear, but a terrain of present manifestation. Solomon is both historical and contemporary, past and present: "I wanted to have a dialogue...I wanted to talk with him." Statements such as "Solomon was concerned about the church" do not carry the shock of anachronism, since Solomon belongs as much to the community gathered this evening as to his ancient kingdom. For the moment he has become an abiding elder.

Solomon's presence is not solely dependent upon language. While nouns such as "church," the use of the present tense, and the direct mode of address all contribute to the understanding of this phenomenon, Salem's religious community is a cultural heir to the religion of the slaves who implored Abraham, Sarah, Jacob, Isaac, Moses, Martha and Mary for strength and guidance.[6] Later in the paper we will also examine the organization of African-American sensibilities in order to better understand the unique character of this religious experience.

[Linda continues:] I wanted to have a talk with him [Solomon] too, because I know he didn't have an easy time. I can only imagine that Solomon had a very difficult time. He had to deal with the same folk that Moses tried to lead into the promised land. These were the church members Moses had standing at the Red Sea. They had freedom in their grasp, and liberty in their eyesight. These were the same folks that told Moses, "Moses, we should have died back in Egypt. We were doing all right with our fleshpots back in the Pharoah's brickyard. At least back in Egypt we had bread, humph, and look, you brought us out here and we're hungry. Back in Egypt we had a balanced budget, because we had no budget. Full employment because we were slaves. And here, Moses, you brought us here with death behind us and hard times ahead of us. Come on, let's go back to Egypt."

Well, you know I feel sort of sorry for Solomon. And I glad I didn't have to face and don't have to face, I pray, those kind of problems. For those with whom he dealt were the direct descendents of the tribes of Israel that finally made it to the Promised Land. Even then, however, when Moses had been there looking over the land which flowed with milk and honey, Caleb and Joshua were the co-chairmen of the committee that went to spy out the land. And he had them at the gateway of God's promise. Folks say, "We're not going." My Bible tells me that the tribe of Reuben, and the tribe of Gad, and half the tribe of Manasseh never made it. They preferred the security of what *used* to be, rather than the glory of what could be. These were the same folk with whom Solomon had to build the temple. And that's why I wanted to have a word with Solomon the King.

It concerns me, and it should concern all of us, and it should interest us *why* Solomon should want to build in the first place. He did not have the resources to build. He had to send 30,000 men to import stones from the quarry of Phoenicia, the wood from the pines and cedars of Lebanon. Solomon ran out of money and he had to take out a second mortgage. And at the same time he was trying to trade off wheat and oil in order to get lumber and gold from Hiram. Solomon needed 8,000 men to build the temple; he needed seven years to complete it.

Now I don't know why Solomon took the risk to build. Because any economist would have told him that he did not have the resources to build. And that's why I wanted to talk with Solomon to find out just what was on his mind when everybody said, "Don't do it."

No doubt Solomon built because he was concerned about the church. And without a *church*, no one would know what Israel thought about their God and the God that they served. And without a *temple*, they would not honor the faith of their fathers, Abraham, Isaac and Jacob. Without a *sanctuary*, there would be no gathering place where the saints of God could praise and pray. Solomon was concerned about the church.

And this leads me to say that we ought to be concerned about the church. I am concerned that unless the church is moving to new vistas of ministry, the creature (that's us) will lose touch with the Creator. I'm concerned that if our persuasion is to live in the past, we shall be no more than curators of ecclesiastical antique shops. We need to be concerned about the church. The church must always be responsive to the age in which it lives. Someone has suggested that the most serious indictment of the contemporary church may be that we are living as citizens of the space age, and at the same time trying to run the church as a horse and buggy operation. Like Solomon, we need to be concerned about the church, because the church is why I can say that a day in the courts is better than a thousand elsewhere. I would rather be a doorkeeper [Alright] in the house of my God than dwell in the tents of wickedness. And so I wanted to *talk* with Solomon tonight, because he may have some instructive insights on this matter of building a house for the Lord.

Now the Bible says, "And the Word of the Lord came to Solomon." And that leads me to say that before you begin to build, you better be certain that you have a Word from the Lord. [Alright] For you see, if you don't, you'll come out here by yourself, and you know it gets pretty lonely sometimes. And if you step out on your own strength well, you'll get weak sometimes. And if you get hung up on your own ego, you'll be hated sometimes. [Uh huh; alright] And don't move off because of your money, because you'll be broke sometimes. If you go, you'd better go because God said, "Go!" The mountains are high and the valleys, we know, are deep; the rivers are so wide and the bridges are broken. Friends, you are few and enemies are many. Interest is high and money is so hard to come by. But I hear Solomon saying, "You'd better be sure you have a Word from the Lord. [Yes] My *Father* told me, "Except the Lord build the house, they labor in vain that build it. Except the Lord keep the city, the watchman waketh in vain." [Alright]

The book says, "the Word of the Lord..." I know you have your architectural design, and I know you have your engineers' specifications. And I know you have made your plans and your projections. But you ought to know something concerning this house that you're about to build.

And so, I wanted to tell you that the first thing that we need to know about building a house for the Lord is that everyone will not want to build...and it's not because they are stubborn, and it's not because they're evil. It's not because they're vindictive. The reason is that a whole lot of folk will want to wait and see what will happen. They want to keep their options open. And they always want to stay away from the possibility of failure, just so they can say, "Huh, I told you so." But when victory comes around they'll be the first to say, "I was with you all the time." [laughter; oh yeah]

I wanted to talk with Solomon, so maybe he could tell us how this house should be built. Solomon suggests that you have to do three things. The first thing you must do is to walk in God's statutes. Now to walk in the statutes means you must be willing to be governed by God's laws. You must be willing to be disciplined by God. The apostle Paul told the Christ at Corinth, "All things must be done decently, and in order." God has some laws. God has some standards of conduct. He has some dictates of discipline.

Now, not only must you walk in his statutes, but God told Solomon, "You have to execute my judgment." You know, we don't like the word "judgment," but I am persuaded by the Holy Spirit, God has a word of judgment for the church. Just because we might look pious, there is still a word of judgment. And never mind how right and righteous we've convinced ourselves that we are, there's still a word of judgment. And it makes no difference how important we look in our uniforms, God *still* has a word of judgment. Jesus went down to the temple—it was the same temple that Solomon is building—and he saw the moneychangers robbing the poor and stealing from the blind.

Jesus told them, "You forgot, this is my house, and it's my Father's house, and my house shall be called a house of prayer. But you, you have made it into a den of thieves."

If we are going to stay away from the judgment of God, there had better be some prayer in this house. The church ought to be a seven-day prayer meeting. Every organization in the church ought to be a prayer meeting. Tithing clubs ought not to tithe until they have prayer meeting. Ushers ought not come to the floor until they have had prayer meeting. [Alright; come on] Choirs ought not to put on their robes until they have had prayer meeting. And deacons ought not to be deacons until they have learned the work of prayer meeting. And the Holy Ghost won't come until there's been a prayer meeting. Solomon prayed, oh yes, he prayed, and God said, "Solomon, I have heard your prayer and your supplication." I don't care what you say, wherever God's home is built, somebody has been praying. You can't build his house unless somebody knows the worth of prayer. Now, I don't know if you know it or not, but I believe that somebody has been praying around here. [Amen] Early Sunday morning, week-in and week-out, somebody has been [Amen] praying around here. Over in the midnight hour, I'm here to tell you *somebody* has been praying. [Yes] And when the darkness of the night has come upon us, you and me, and when we toss and turn and we can't sleep, I'm telling you, *somebody's* been praying. [Oh yes] And somebody's been praying around here [rising inflection], because *somebody* said, "Father, I stretch my hands to thee, no other help I know." [Well]

And so the record says, "When Solomon had finished building the house of the Lord, the Lord appeared to Solomon the second time." For you see, when God has work for you to do, He not only appears one time, but He comes a second time. And I might offer that I wouldn't move to build a house for the Lord if He has not revealed it to you. If the Lord doesn't reveal it a first time, He will not be back a second time. And so, here we stand on the threshold of an opportunity to build again.

And the Holy Spirit moved upon our pastor some five or six years ago, to reveal to him the land upon which we are to build. And at that time the land was $500,000 or more; we didn't have it, and we had no vision as to how to get it. But God has come around a second time. The land now is $123,000. God has come around a second time.

For you see when he reveals his work, the first time He assigns you, the second time He confirms you. The first time He gives you sight, but the second time He gives you insight. The first time He reveals His plan, but the second time he reveals His purpose. When he appeared to Moses the first time, He said, "Put off thy shoes from off thy feet for the place whereon thy standeth is holy ground." But when he appeared to Moses the second time He said, "Tell Pharaoh, 'Let my people go.'" The first time He appeared to Isaiah, He showed his political power, kingly pomp, and regal pageantry. But the second time He appeared, Isaiah said, "In the year King Uziah died I saw also the Lord high and lifted up." The first time He appeared to Ezekiel, all he could see was the dry bones in a valley. "And lo, they were very dry." But the second time He appeared to Ezekiel, all he could see was dry bones connecting one by one, and a wheel in the middle of a wheel. The first time He appeared to John, it was on an isle called Patmos, and all he could see was the loneliness of isolation, and the prison cell of solitary confinement. But the second time He appeared to John, John saw something else when he said, "I saw a new heaven and a new earth coming down out of heaven as a bride adorned for her husband." The first time He appeared to Solomon at Gideon, Solomon asked for an understanding heart. But the second time the Lord appeared, He said, "Solomon, I have hallowed this house which you have built." And I just thought you ought to know that if it's God's will, He will appear a second time.

Linda's illustrations here serve less as an argument than as a means of enrolling both the church's leadership and the allegiance of its members into the realm of divine workings, to make the people of faith one people with one plan: God's.

And so God has revealed His will, and He's appeared a second time. And as Christians and stewards of all that He gives us, He is going to hold us accountable with what we do, and with how we carry out this latest assignment. As a race, we are confronted on every side with the *maladies of our society*. People are hurting, they are lonely, they are lost. Many of our elderly are forced to live out their golden years as paupers, as lonely. There are many young families who need training and re-training so that they can survive in the 21st century. And our youth, yes, our youth need sanctuary of refuge, where they can be taught the difference between good and evil. Where Christian morals, again, can become the foundation upon which they can build their lives. The Word says, "To whom much is given, much will be required." And Salem, God has confirmed the work that we must do. As members of this church, God has assembled us together at this particular point in time so that He can weld together our gifts, our talents and our resources. All of those things which He has given to us concerning this house, the brickmason will put it together with mortar, but God will put it together with mercy. The quarry will provide the stones, but God will be the chief cornerstone. The contractor will work by blueprints, but God has a divine design. The structure will be welded with steel, but the superstructure is the plan of salvation. The engineer will study the strength of the structure, but the God we serve was here before the hills in order stood, and long before the earth received her frame. [Yes] The draftsman will say, "Build it on the rock foundation," but the Great Architect of the Universe has said, "Build it on the Word."

And so, Solomon built the house and he finished it. He didn't just start it, he finished it. He didn't just break ground for it, he finished it. And he didn't just talk about it, but he finished it. Thank you. [Amen; umm-hmm; vigorous applause]

[Solo]:
Like the woman at the well
I was seeking for things that could not satisfy
But I heard my Savior speaking
He said, Draw from my well that never shall run dry
[That's right]
Like the millions in the world, I was seeking
For earthly pleasures, like a fire
But none can match these wondrous pleasures
That I found in Christ Jesus, my, my Lord
Oooohhh, fill my cup Lord [Alright]
I lift it up to Thee
Come and quench this thirst from my soul
Bread of heaven, feed me till I want no more
Lord, fill my cup, fill it up and make me whole
Oooohhh, Fill my cup, Lord
I lift it up to Thee
Come and quench this thirst from my soul
Bread of heaven, feed me till I want no more
Lord, fill my cup, fill it up and make me whole
Oooohhh, Fill my cup, Lord
I lift it up to Thee [Oh yes He can]
Fill my cup Lord, fill my cup Lord, fill my cup, Lord
I lift it up to Thee

Come and quench this thirst from my soul
Bread of heaven, fill me till I want no more
Lord, fill my cup, fill it up, fill it up, fill it up
And make me whole

[Rev. Sypho]: Most of us, we try to fill that desire with the emptiness
of this world, but I stopped by tonight, Salem, to tell you that the
world can't satisfy you, but I know a man who is able to satisfy each
and every one of us. The Bible says that Jesus was down at the well
one day, and he asked a woman for a drink of water, and He told her,
he said, "If you knew who I was." You see, it depends on who you
know; don't always depend upon what you know, but who you know.
Jesus said, "If you knew who I was, I could give you a drink of water,
that you'd never thirst no more, huh, it'd be like a well springing up
inside. I don't know about you [laughs] but I had a drink [laughs]
and it wasn't long ago [laughs]. I don't know about you, but I'm just
glad about it. Jesus has still got that water. And when you get tired
of everything else, when you get tired of the rest, you want to try the
best, try Jesus. God bless you.

There are some here this evening that God has done something for,
and you need to tell it. [Tell it] You can save some strength by
knowing that you've gone through it, and when I see that you've
gone through it, then I'm able to go through it, and somebody behind
them are able to go through it, and somebody behind them are able to
go through it, and when we look back, you know what, heaven won't
be so lonely [laughs]. We'll really be able to say, "Howdy, howdy."
They'll be no more goodbyes. Somebody come, please.

Linda Perkins, who has just delivered the interpretive conversation
with Solomon, walks forward. This time she stands before the
members not as a teacher but as a fellow sufferer, in need of prayer and
affirmation. Testimony is an act of obedience. It is a personal story of
God's activity in the recent past, placing the event within one ("placed
in the heart") during the act of telling. Testimony is no longer a
report, but an event. God becomes active in the present moment,
moving in the congregation's spiritual response. The telling of a prior
event creates a new event of equal importance, for this event becomes
an experience for others. Something happens in the course of her
testimony. Linda experiences God's *power* in the midst of her
vulnerability.

Giving honor to God, I have to share this testimony, because I
promised the Lord that whatever He did for me, I would stand in the
congregation and say my vows. [pause]

I'm self-employed and you know, it gets hard. It's hard enough when you work on a job every day, and you know you have a paycheck coming in every week or every two weeks. But when you're self-employed, you don't know when the paycheck is coming. [My Lord] But if God has given you something to do as I know He has done for me, then you go on anyway. And it gets real rough sometimes. Sometimes I feel like I'm just about ready to cave in. And sometimes I stand and say, "Lord is it worth it all?" But then He has a way of comforting you. [voice weakening] And say, "Just stay on, 'cause I'm gonna make it alright."

I was in a car accident about two years ago. I was on my back for almost a year. Getting up behind that, being self-employed, it's been rough! [voice amplifying] Trying to get back into the grind of things. Earlier this year I had some contracts I had worked on. I hadn't got paid. I called and they said, "Well, Linda, uh the Governor—it's over in the Governor's office, and it got lost in the papers, it's got to be submitted again, and blah, blah, blah, blah."

You know they give you the run-around. I said, "OK." So every month for the last eight or nine months I been calling. And I said all that to say, I've been waiting on my payment. That which is due me, and I haven't received it yet. But the other day, I went to the mailbox and looked in. There was a letter from the insurance company. And I said, "Ooohhh Lord, what's wrong now?"

And something told me—it was the Holy Spirit—to go in the house. So I went in the house and it said, "Open it up." And I opened it up and inside there was a letter that says: "Dear Ms. Perkins, In researching our records, we find that we miscalculated on the settlement, and so herewith enclosed is a check for X amount of dollars." You see, I had been praying, and I asked God—you know Pastor [Williams] said, "Send up an emergency prayer," and I said, "Well, Lord, you know the rent is due, the phone is due, this person's due and that person is due, and I don't know where it's *coming* from... [Well, I know what you talking 'bout] But I had promised that I would *live* for Him... My gifts and my talents I would *use* for Him... [Say it] [voice rising] And I tried to *use* them and I *thanked* Him all along, I said, "Lord, thank you for what little knowledge you've given me. Thank you for the *skill* that you've given me. And if you let me use it, I'll continue to *praise your name.*"

I almost tore up my living room. And I find it difficult to stand here now because [pause] *it might not come when you want it* [each word spoken with weighted deliberation; members begin to stir; chorus of "oh yes, yes"; hand claps] *but it's always*...believe me when I tell you...*it's always* [voice cracking, applause increasing] *on time.* And it might not *come* the way you *think* it should come, and from the *source* you think it will come, but I'm here to tell you tonight that if you hang on [Yeah], if you're *dedicated* to him [people standing], if you *live* for Him... [That's right] *I'm a living witness*!!! [Yeah] He'll work it out for *you*. [shouted tearfully]: Hallelujah!!! [Vigorous applause; yes Lord; that's alright; that's what we need, that what we need]

Rev. Sypho]: Is God real? How many of you know He's real? [applause, hands raised as signs of the spirit's presence] [piano accompaniment] I don't know about you, but He's been real to me. Jesus is real. If you don't believe He's real, then try Him. If you don't believe Him [bends down], every now and then, go down on your knees. You see I got up this morning with my mind stayed on Jesus. See, nobody asked me to testify. I got a testimony this morning. Woo!! [Amen, hallelujah]

[Rev. Sypho]: Will there be another testimony? Yeah. Praise the Lord. Come on, brother, you come on too. That's what's wrong with all of us, now we suppose to be saints and we ashamed just to say, "Thank You, Jesus." Oh my Lord.

[Woman comes forward weeping]
[Rev. Sypho]: That's alright, Momma, take your time, take your time.
[Woman]: Good evening everybody. [Good evening] I don't have very much to say. But I just know God is real. [Yes] I have a little problem I been working on. I haven't said anything to nobody, but I've just been mumbling it to myself and asking God about it. 'Cause I know, if it wasn't for the Lord, what would I do? I prayed about it. I've restless nights over it. I've called this one and I've called that one. And I've just been in a turn-around. Every time I've called one person, they'd send me to another one. Every time I'd call this next, they'd send me to another one. And I just didn't know what to do about it, so I just fell down and give it up. Well, I decided within myself, prayer changes things. [Yes it does, yeah]

The response is determined by the nature of the testimony. Here the situation was unresolved. The congregation's affirmation was directed toward her faith in the midst of the difficulty in which she still lived.

[Woman begins weeping] They say it's never been a problem that God was not able to solve. [Yes; say it] [laughter from Rev. Sypho] [Ooo-hhh; umm-hmm]

I know that I been to the river [umm-hmm], and I been baptized. I stepped in the water [Yes], and I come out alright. [Yes] And I want to thank the Lord for it because it wasn't me, now. [Well] It's God. He set me, He brought me, and He did these things for me. I been down there, I been down there. But I didn't worry about being down there, because I know the Lord was with me, and He's going to bring me out of it. So I just kept on a-praying, and I just kept on a-mumbling over it, and I just kept on a-praying on it. My daughter said one night, "Momma, I just get so tired of you just mumbling over things, you just...blup blup blup blup blup." She didn't know what I was saying. But I was just talking to the Lord. And I didn't say nothing to her, I just looked at her, 'cause I know she didn't know. 'Cause God is real, and that He have all power in His hands. But I'm here to tell you tonight, I *do* believe that God will solve my problems. [Amen; applause]

[Young man's testimony]: Good evening everyone. Umm. This is my first time ever testifying. But I thank God for being here and being able to testify. Because I have a lot to be grateful for. For 26 years I thought it was me. I was used to that old slogan, "I did everything, I was responsible for this, I was responsible for that." But I'm here to tell you. Life, I felt, was great for me. I had gone through undergraduate school. I had got my master's, had this great job, but something was missing. I *didn't* know what I wanted. I wanted something, but I didn't know what I wanted. And, having been part of a former religion–I was a Catholic–and uh, I don't knock Catholicism, but I just didn't find it there. [Oh my Lord]

So I got my first touch in terms of trying to seek and find, while attending undergraduate school. And while I was there, I sang in a choir, and it was a gospel choir, and we sang at Baptist and Methodist churches throughout the weekends. At any rate, that was my first encounter with something different as opposed to Catholicism. One part of me found the Lord in a way through music, but I didn't know how to respond to that. And just as our beloved lady said, "He comes more than once." [Hmm, alright] So that was way back in 1984. He brought me up to 1989. I still hadn't found it. But thanks to His Grace, I did find it. [Amen in chorus]

I just celebrated my 27th birthday. But it's not because of the birth, my physical birthday. I thank God for being born again. [Amen; applause] I thank God because on this birthday, I had through His Grace, and through the love of my family back in Maryland–because I've only been here for a month–anyway I found Him. I'm 27 years old, and the first days... I feel like I'm crawling. I'm still learning, and I feel good about testifying, I have to tell you that. [applause] I've always been scared, but I always knew I had something to say, or serious–say something. For you see, nothing terrible, nothing bad has happened. It's that I didn't know where I was going. It wasn't money, it wasn't this, it wasn't that. And what others may feel is great, in terms of worldly things, you would have thought I would have been happy. Which was hard for my family to accept or understand initially. Because they couldn't understand, "Why are you thinking...?" But I always thought about joining a Baptist church. I thought about it because the music and because the preaching attracted me. But then when I understood the Word and then started hearing the Word, the Lord made it a part of my heart and [Amen] everything else, the reason changed. And once that changed, I could express it more, I could feel it more. And now my family is so happy for me. And I prayed for them, that they'll find Jesus the way I did. [Amen; yes]

So you don't need to have everything going wrong. [Amen] You don't need to have something just bad [applause], because things were good as I thought, but they weren't–because I just needed something else. What was in this world, the money, and anything else I had physically, was not good enough, love–that just wasn't...I needed Jesus. [My God; extended applause] And I thank God for that. And I'm here to tell you, I don't know how but I thank God that I kept holding on [Yes sir], that I kept praying on, that I kept singing on. And I ask your prayer for me, and I pray the Lord tonight that I keep holding on and praying on so that I can be able to witness better, that I can be a better Christian, so I can get to learn 'cause see, I'm new at this. Not just that talking–I have to learn the Word. For years I was told the Word, now I have to receive it in my heart and my mind. [Aha! laughter, applause] And Salem, thank God for you, because I joined the church and there was one...I saw her come in, she was part of my orientation and I joined the church and she's been great just talking with her and seeing her–she just made a difference. She's sitting way in the back with the lady who sang [laughs]. But anyway, Salem is great and I thank God for Salem [Amen], and I pray that while I'm here I do my work, I mean God's work. [Amen; applause]

[Rev. Sypho]: Now as we go to the throne of Grace, I guess that being in the position that I am in, that I'm a little bit closer to Pastor Williams than most. [piano plays supportive, plaintive chords beneath his speaking] You know, a lot of times I watch the struggle, dedication, the sincerity of him giving himself to the Lord. And I said many times in this great place, this great church, "Lord, teach us how to be good followers." You see, because a leader is no greater than the people he's leading. And whenever a shepherd leads a group of people, and they constantly stay in prayer, asking the Lord to give them strength, and to give the shepherd strength, power comes after the saints have beseeched the throne of God. Tonight I want all of us to stand and join hands all across the chapel. And I want you to pray, and I want you to pray honestly. I want everyone in here to ask the Lord to let His will be done in your life. Not according to what *you* want, but ask God to let His will be done. If it's a bad habit, ask the Lord to help you to drop that habit. If it's a problem, ask Him to help you deal with the problem. Salem, I am a living witness that God will hear and answer prayer. [Yes Lord]

Every head bowed, every eye closed. Every heart opened unto God. Pray for those things which you stand in need of, and pray for your church family. Pray for our government, pray for our teenagers. Pray for the auxiliaries in which you work. Ask God to bind you together with strength, with Holy Ghost power that He and only He alone is able to give. You talk to him tonight, saints. You can either pray silent, or you can pray aloud. But I'm thankful to God tonight that I'm not ashamed of the Gospel of Jesus Christ. [piano accompaniment]

[Rev. Sypho sings]:
I need Thee, oh I need Thee,
Every hour I need Thee
Oh bless me now my Saviour
I come to, to Thee
I need Thee, oh I need Thee
Every hour I need thee
Oh bless me now, my Saviour
I come to, to Thee
Oh I need Thee, oh I need Thee
Every hour more I need Thee
Oh bless, oh bless, oh bless, me now
my Saviour
I come to Thee

[Rev. Sypho's prayer]: Our Father and our God, Lord, here we are again, gathered together one more time in your name. First of all recognizing and understanding, Lord, that we are sinners, we've said and done things that were contrary to Your Word and Your will. We've gone on to do things that were ungodly. And we come tonight before Thee, asking, Father, that Thou would cleanse us of all our sins. Help us, Father, as we walk this path of righteousness. Oh God, now as we look out, Lord Jesus, and see those, Lord Jesus, who have come. Some who have come, Lord Jesus, need one thing and others, yet another. Some come crying, "I need prayer because I'm sick," and Lord, we come asking that you would heal the sick tonight. Then, Father, some come crying, "I need direction," and we come asking tonight for direction. And then, Lord, some come crying, saying, "we're weak and we're tore down," and we ask tonight, God, that You build them up where they're tore down, and build them up where they're weak, Lord. We know tonight, huh, that if You look, huh, the lame will be made whole. Those who were unlearned will become learned. Tonight, Lord, those who don't bear will be able to bear, huh, if You look tonight, Lord, those who are hungry can be fed. Huh, if You look tonight, Lord, those who need, huh, will no longer be in need. If You look tonight, Father, we know that You can look down from heaven, that You can dispatch the angels from heaven, huh, that You can answer every one of our problems, huh, that You can solve all of our needs, huh, that You can give us whatever we need from the bank in glory, huh, created by Christ Jesus, huh, and we come tonight, Lord, huh, knowing that You're no shorter than Your Word, huh, that You're able to keep us, huh, from falling, huh, and to present us faultless before Your glory with exceeding joy, huh. [higher, singing pitch, wail-like] We *thank* You tonight, God, huh, that things are as well as they are, huh. We *thank* You tonight, Lord, huh, that You let us come together one more time. You see, we don't know what tomorrow holds, huh, but we know tonight that if we just call on Your name, huh, that everything will be alright. [Yes]

Now Lord [Now Lord], Now Lord [Now Lord] we come asking, Father, that You would touch those, Lord Jesus, who are sick and afflicted. We pray, Father, for those who are home-bound. We pray, Father, for our pastor, and we pray for the youth of our church. We pray constantly for the government. We pray, Lord Jesus, for families, that they may continue to be what they ought to be. We pray, Lord Jesus, for young Christians; we pray for old Christians. We pray, Father, that Your Word may penetrate our hearts and minds. Let us be better servants. Let us be doers of the Word, and not hearers only. Oh God, we just pray Your magnifying blessing. We pray that You would just use us until You use us up. And we'll be careful to give Your name all the praise, the honor and the glory, until we meet in that final hour, in that great getting-up morning, when we shall all be able, Lord Jesus, to sing: "How I got over." [Yeah] We thank You, we praise You [Well] in the name of Jesus, in the name of Jesus [louder], in the name of Jesus [louder], in the name of Jesus [louder still], Amen. [piano]

[Rev. Sypho]: We are going to ask quickly that anyone who has an announcement, that you come forward, and we ask that the deacons would get ready for our offering.

[Ida]: I come before you for a personal request from one of the members... All of you may know ___. She is expecting, doctors have announced they think there is something wrong with the child. She called and she said to me, "Ida, take it to the church. I want the church to pray for my child." She says, "I'm not worried about myself, but I just want the baby to be all right... and ask the church to please remember us in their prayers." [Amen]

An invitation is extended for members of the congregation to pray with the woman. Then an announcement is made by the Social Services Ministries regarding living arrangements: a business woman wants someone to share her home, and an older woman living alone needs a housemate. Referrals are made for people who need help with their utilities.

> [Rev. Sypho]: "Amen. I'd just like to remind all of us that on Sunday we all ought to be in uniform the first Sunday because we will be issuing the Lord's Supper."

After other announcements are made and the offering collected, Rev. Sypho addresses the members, who are still standing, and instructs them to "Shake your neighbor's hand, and just tell 'em [sings]:

> Thank You Lord, Thank You Lord, Thank You Lord.
>   [members join in]:
>   I just want to thank You Lord.
> And because He's been so good...
>   Praise Your name
> Come on saints, let me hear you say it.
>   Praise Your name
>   Praise Your name
>   I just want to praise Your name
> Thank You Lord. Come on help me say it...
>   Thank You Lord
> There's somebody standing on the outside that didn't come to prayer meeting...
>   Thank you Lord
>   I just want to thank you Lord
> One more time!
>   Praise Your name
>   Praise Your name
>   Praise Your name
>   I just want to praise Your name
> Let's give the Lord a handclap of praise.

Chapter 3

Sunday Worship Service

Context

Every worship service at Salem follows the same basic structure. The three-part sequence consists of:
I.   Deacon's Devotion
II.   Choir and Congregational Singing and Prayers
III.   Pastor's Service: Bible Lesson, Sermon, Invitation to Church Membership

Each of these major sections of the service has a different leader. The morning devotions are under the collective leadership of the deacons; the choir and congregational service is led by Rev. Sypho; and the third section is the responsibility of Pastor Williams.

It is important to keep in mind that a number of those who attend the Wednesday night prayer meetings are also present for early morning devotions. The Salem community is created out of numerous cellular communities whose members move between multiple intra-church organizations. The Wednesday night prayer warriors are joined by the Sunday morning saints, many of whom are the elderly (of both sexes) whose consistent attendance is a measure both of their reliance upon the strength which emerges in the act of praying, and of their commitment to the welfare of the entire community.

Deacon's Devotion

The deacon's devotion is collective. Deacons are individual leaders who pray for the entire country. As the deacon speaks for the collective, the personal dies. While the deacon's devotion stands as a distinct and complete religious ritual, the activities, which precede and follow it, help to define it in the life of the church.

Members start to arrive before 10:00 a.m. in order to attend one of the many Bible studies conducted at various sites throughout the church. The members greet one another with warmth and enthusiasm, expressing concern and making inquiries about each other's daily condition. The women make compliments on each other's personal attire. Admiring questions about hair, style and coiffeur are interlaced with remarks about figure and weight. While the men are less given to topics of personal grooming, sartorial elegance does not go unnoticed as they amend their greetings with statements such as, "Looking sharp this morning, Brother Robinson."

Extensive time is devoted to simply admiring the children of the church, all of whom are neatly dressed, well-groomed, displaying the hours of parental investment needed to obtain this magnificence in miniature. One can hear the frequently repeated phrase, "Give me some sugar!" addressed to a young child as a prelude to a shower of kisses and hugs bestowed upon them by female elders.

While much of the exchange between members who gather in the narthex before Bible study or worship seems to be characterized by casual purposelessness, these encounters are shaped by the intentional character of nurturant affirmation. I will return to this topic below in the section on phenomenological interpretation. At this point I only want to stress that while this activity occurs in response to members' personal needs, appearance, an outstanding solo or choir performance, or a function well executed, the overall tenor of concern and edifying remarks is evoked not by *achievement* but simply because one is present. In other words, the conditions which motivate nurturant affirmation and response are highly unconditional.

Leaving the narthex to enter the nave, one changes one's demeanor, conversation, and orientation. The tone and volume of speaking becomes muted. The alteration is not the result of standing in the presence of a sacred object or site, such as one would observe in the behavior of those who come into the presence of the alter or tabernacle in a Catholic church. Salem has no pieces of immovable sacred furniture or permanently demarcated holy place. The sanctuary is even without a crucifix. Yet one senses an atmospheric claim upon one's reverential sensibilities.

Salem is one of the truly well-designed churches I have attended, where style of architecture and style of worship are thoroughly integrated. Rather than the typical plan, the Protestant-style rectangle, Salem is constructed like an amphitheater with pews that radiate concentrically in ever-widening arcs toward the balcony. The rear of the nave is therefore a wide concave wall. The longest and widest pews are closest to this wall, with each succeeding pew slightly shorter than the one behind it, each with the same degree of curvature. The floor of the sanctuary is built upon a descending grade. Each of the six aisles moves toward the apex of the chancel, a point located right behind the pulpit. All lines converge upon the place of prominence commanded by the pastor, or whoever is presiding. Instead of turning to view the pastor, one is automatically positioned and focused upon him as long as he stays within the pulpit area. Upon entering the sanctuary, one is literally pulled toward this focal point by the floor's incline. Physically and visually one is drawn toward the center of activity and attention.

Members who enter move toward this center without the encouragement of ushers or the exhortation of ministers. These members want to be as close as possible to the deacon's devotion. With its enormous size, equipped with a balcony and vaulted ceiling, Salem is a commodious church. The isles are carpeted in a warm maroon-beige, and the pews are cushioned on the back and the seat in a soft blue. Both carpeting and padding dampen the sound of movement and conversation, giving the sanctuary's acoustics a more intimate quality. Given the radiating design, the devoted chancel has a smaller diameter than the rest of the sanctuary. The focus of the congregation's attention, therefore, contributes to the spatial closeness.

Salem's decor is posh but not lavish. The church is definitely moving toward up-scale attainments, and while the congregation is noticeably on the higher end, they have not tilted toward the garish.

In contrast to the comfortable finery of the furniture, a single drab grey metal folding chair stands alone in the space immediately in front of the pulpit. The chair appears all the uglier in its stark inharmonious coarseness of color and shape. As the members settle into silence, Deacon Napper stands and turns toward the members. He is dressed in the conservative cloth of his office: a dark grey wool suit, conservatively cut without concession to modern stylishness. Deacon Napper is president of the Deacon Board, one of the church elders, and a highly respected person within Salem's hierarchy and community. His gifts as a leader, both spiritual and organizational, are extremely important to the life of the church and, as we shall see, to its vitality of worship.

Napper holds an open hymnal containing selections, which are known individually as "a Dr. Watts." The collected hymns of this early eighteenth century English evangelist became very popular among primitive Afro-American Christians during the Great Awakening of the same century. They are sung *a cappella* in a variety of tempi, which makes them versatile and applicable in a number of settings. They are the preferred hymns among the older members of the church. The

Watts hymnal is well suited for these services, not only because many
of the members are older (though there are a significant number of
younger and middle-aged people also present), but also because the
music is choral and lends itself to the untutored harmonies of congregational singing. These hymns yield to the flexible contours of Black
vocal creativity since they have long and elastic lines.

Deacon Napper begins "lining" a hymn, singing the first verse,
followed by the congregation entering the song; he then talks the
second verse, followed by singing. He is the only one with a hymnal,
leaving everyone else free to focus upon him and the singing. The
hymns are never posted in advance since the leader often selects them
according to the mood and needs of the moment. The leader is given
the latitude to order and adapt the service to the immediate context.
The distinction between rite as a pre-existent *text* which is enacted, and
an extemporized service, will be considered below in the interpretive
section of the book.

Deacon Napper speaks: "Father, I stretch my hand to thee, no other
help I know." The members join him: "Father, I stretch my hand to
thee, no-o-o-o other help...I know." Deacon Napper: "If Thou withdraw Thyself from me, Ah! whither shall I go?" The congregation
repeats the line, but richly altered.

The members know this prayerful anthem intimately. Charles Wes-
ley's hymn is a standard part of Black hymnals. It is worth
considering why this selection commands the allegiance of Black
Christians across denominational boundaries. This question will be
addressed formally in the latter section of this book. For now, the full
text is included since Deacon Napper chose to include all four stanzas:

Father, I stretch my hands to Thee,
No other help I know;
If Thou withdraw Thyself from me,
Ah! whither shall I go?

What did Thine only Son endure
Before I drew my breath!
What pain, what labor, to secure
My soul from endless death!

Surely Thou canst not let me die;
O speak, and I shall live;
And here I will unwearied lie,
'Til Thou Thy Spirit give.

Author of faith! to Thee I lift
My weary, longing eyes;

O let me not receive that gift!
My soul without it dies. Amen.
        —Charles Wesley

As the congregation musically responds to Deacon Napper, the other deacons, who have been seated in the first pew, stand.   One has removed his suit coat before rising, and he is approached by his fellow deacons who begin to shake and grasp his hands.   Each of the six deacons repeat this gesture with the divested deacon.   As this ceremony proceeds, Deacon Napper makes a gesture and the gathered members rise, still singing.   Once everyone is standing, and the deacons have completed the rite of preparation, the designated individual kneels before the metal chair which faces the pulpit.   He is in a position facing the congregation, resting his elbows on the seat of the chair. When he is settled at his station, Deacon Napper signals the congregation to be seated.   They sing a few more words from the verse before growing silent.   The church is hushed.   Into this silent sanctuary emerges the sonority of a voice full of pleading and praise.

Father, we come before You suffering need, one more time.
After bowing down this morning, not bowing for form or fashion, I'm not bowing down for outside show to the world.
I'm bowing down because You said every knee would bow.
You said that every tongue would confess.
We're bowing down to take time to thank You, Master, thank You, oh God, for our lying down last night, for sending down Your guardian angel.
He watched over us all night long while we lied down, clutching to our self.
You kept the blood running warm in our veins.
We just want to say thank You, oh Master, You been so *good* to us.
You been better to us than we been to ourselves.
And Lord, we pray right this morning, I know that You hear our prayer this morning, O-o-oh Lord, O-o-oh Lord, I know we get weak some time, but You make us strong.
I know sometime the way get dark, I know You be the light on the pathway.
Sometime our mountain get high, I know You're the ladder to the highest mountain, O-o-oh Lord, O-o-oh Lord.
I know You not hard of hearing this morning.
I want You to get in Pastor Williams this morning, make his word be progressing to and fro.
Come singing on the right and on the left, O-o-oh Lord, O-o-oh Lord.
I know somebody didn't feel like coming [individual claps] this morning, but they came on in Your name.

You said, "If I be lifted upon the breath that You draw al-l-l unto You this morning, O-o-oh Lord, O-o-oh Lord.
When I prayed my last prayer, and when I've sung my last song, and when I'm through [unintelligible] my [unintelligible] and I can't fight them no more, give me a ho-o-ome, h-o-o-ome, ah, over yonder, where every day will be sunny and prayer will have no end.
Praise everlasting in Jesus' name, Amen! Thank God.

As this prayer develops, the congregation responds in a variety of ways. The interactions are rhythmic, entering into the pauses between the verses, wedding rhythmic propulsion to the deacon's prayer. The interjections are: "Amen; That's right; Yes Lord; Have mercy." The other deacons continue to sing a counter-melody to the songful prayer chant of Deacon Napper. Theirs is an elongated melody which rises and falls, ending as the deacon's prayer concludes.

On the rhythmic beat immediately following his prayer, Deacon Napper begins singing "Amazing Grace."

How sweet the sound, oh yeah,
That saved a wretch like me.
I once was lost but now I'm found,
...blind but now I see.
T'was grace that taught my heart to fear
And grace my fears relieved,
How precious did that grace appear
The hour I first believed.
T'was grace, nothing but grace,
that taught my heart to fear.

Deacon Napper repeats the second stanza. The congregation joins in immediately, before Deacon Napper has completed the first line. This hymn is so well known and closely identified with the church that many members are unaware that John Newton, an eighteenth century British captain of merchant ships transporting human cargo from Africa, composed the hymn.

The deacon's devotion is far more thematic and inclusive of community, less specific and individual than the prayers found within the Wednesday night prayer meeting. The prayer meeting is far more personal while the Sunday service deacon's devotion speaks in the voice of the collective ("we," "some"). At the prayer meeting "Jesus" is far more likely to be addressed along with "God," while "Father" is the exclusive subject addressed in the deacons' service. The deacon's devotion does not include the struggles rooted in the specific situations which individual members bring before the congregation in their testimony. The whole congregation stands, along with the deacons, as the designated prayer descends to the foot of the cross, marked by the metal folding chair.

[Deacon Napper shouts]: Pray, Salem, come on!
[Continues singing:]
Set your heart to Jesus
I am bound to glorify the God
Who gave His son my soul to save and fit it for the sky,
To save this present age, my calling to fulfill.
May all my power engage, I said my all, I'm going to do my Master's will.
[Shouts]: You just can't stop the spirit!
[Continues singing]:
Our Father, Our Father, Our Father,
which art in heaven,
Hallowed by Thy name, Thy kingdom come
and let Thy will be done
on earth as it is in heaven.
And then, oh Father, you brought us all to your house of worship one more time,
[Pray Salem!]
And you said, on your child that men must always pray
that Our Father, Our Father, pray that early, early this morning, you touched me, and you told me to get up...
It wasn't judgment morning.
But since I has rose, I came out to the house of worship
and I have listened to a portion of your chant and hymn song
and the worship touched me and told me to go down on my afflicted bended knees one more time.
And to Thee, oh Father, we have come eleven months and a few days to 1989.
We might not make it to see 19 hundred 99
but I pray, oh Father, that someone, someone has gone on to the other side of judgment, that someone has been sick for days, some has years, and some has many, many months [Oh God], but we pray, oh Father [Pray hard], oh Lord, have mercy on us today.
But we didn't come this far ourselves but grace has carried us this far, and I'm talking about Amazing Grace, Amazing Grace, how sweet the sound that saved a wretch like me.
I once was lost but now I'm found, blind but now I see. I was through many, many dangers, toils and snares, but oh, I have already come [Yes sir], heavenly grace has brought us, and if you'll never, never hear me again, I want y'all to meet me.
I wanna go home on the morning train, the evening train may be too late, but this little prayer to the cross, but this is our prayer to the cross and Bible, Lord.

The sanctuary is filled at this point; pews are swollen with members who respect the sanctity of the moment, but wary of its power, approach cautiously and in silence.

[Deacon Napper sings]: I'm not worried 'bout my soul, oh Lord
[congregation]: I'm not worried 'bout my soul, I'm not...
[Deacon Napper]: Oh well... I fixed it
[congregation]: Oh well... I fixed it with Jesus, oh, 'long time ago.
[Deacon Napper]: Well I'm ...
[congregation]: ...not worried 'bout my soul
[Deacon Napper]: Well, I'm not worried 'bout my soul, Lord, I'm not...
[congregation]:... worried 'bout my soul
[Deacon Napper]: O-o-oh, I fixed with Jesus, 'long time ago.
[congregation]: O-o-oh, I'm not worried 'bout my soul
[Deacon Napper speaks]: Sure 'nuff, Salem, I'm not worried about it.
[organ begins to play]
[Rev. Sypho laughs]: 's alright, Brother Napper.
[Choir procession enters in black and white robes]

Choir and Congregational Singing and Prayers

The transition from the deacon's devotion to the congregational worship is eased by the organ prelude. The music is both dulcet and rhapsodic, usually improvised, full of extended phrases with intermittent bursts and flourishes. For those who are already seated, the prelude provides an atmosphere conducive to meditation and reflection. Members who have been waiting in the narthex during the deacon's devotion are allowed to enter and take their seats. Rev. Sypho and Rev. Lewis, who made their ascent to the chancel during Deacon Napper's last hymn, have taken their assigned places. Rev. Sypho, as the pastor's executive assistant, sits to the stage right of the pastor's throne, Rev. Lewis to the left. They are the only two people who will share this space with the pastor. Together, they frame the empty chair and space to be occupied by the pastor. Pastor Williams' chair is slightly larger, the back slightly higher than the other two. Its emptiness is intensified by the occupancy of the adjacent seats, and functions to direct the focus of the congregation's expectations toward the pastor's anticipated arrival.

Salem's Mass Choir, over 85 members strong, processes down the aisles. Once in place, the assemblage of pleated black and white robes forms a tableau in striking contrast to the softer colors of the sanctuary. The choir members command attention and signal to the congregation that the next phase of worship is ready to commence. The young director, Leon, emerges from behind the choir loft. His hair is cut in the contemporary fashion known in the Black community as a "fade." He stands motionless before the choir. The organ, piano and drums begin a lively, up-tempo number.

The choir director explodes into leaping gesticulation. A wall of sound rolls forth from the black and white tapestry. The saxophone joins the ensemble, the congregation clapping in rhythm; the house is alive.

The form of gospel music, in sharp contrast to the mournful hymns and prayers, addresses a different set of religious sensibilities. This is the electrically amplified pulse of the technological metropolis. The rhythms measured by breath and sounds shaped by suffering in the deacon's devotion took form in a pre-industrial, rural terrain. The high energy orchestrated and rehearsed music of contemporary gospel does not completely erase the acoustic dimensions of the earlier stage of the worship. Rather, like the rude metal chair which marked the presence and power of an awesome deity, but has not been folded and placed out of sight, the sensibility and sanctity evoked earlier are enfolded and displaced, only to re-emerge transformed at another point of entry into the service.

This particular piece also allows those who arrived during the deacon's devotion, but were not part of it, to enter a shared mood. The dirge-like hymns which were in progress as large numbers arrived were inaccessible to the recent arrivals. The up-tempo gospel feeling is far lighter and more porous, allowing people both to participate and to search for their seats without interrupting the over-all mood.

The first choir number completed, Rev. Sypho steps forward to the pulpit. The entire congregation rises. Rev. Sypho inquires, "What did we come to do?"

"Worship the Lord," Salem answers.

Rev. Sypho then reads the Call to Worship in a commanding voice, setting a tone of grandeur. The "Gloria Patri" follows, which the congregation knows by heart; the choir joins. The slow, majestic hymn of praise is filled with long lines that require plenty of wind. With over a thousand voices singing full tilt, the climax is thunderous. One hears and feels the reverberations resounding throughout the sanctuary floor, pews and atmosphere. While still standing, Rev. Sypho invites the members to sing the congregational hymn "There is a Fountain." The hymn is printed in the bulletin so that the continuity of singing is not interrupted by people fumbling for hymnals, stooping over, and searching for page numbers. The congregation enters the familiar melody with ease, while many sing the verses from memory. Celebrating the sacrifice of Jesus and the consequent forgiveness of sins, the hymn is invigorating and mood-lifting. Singing all five verses sustains the mood. Members are clapping and moving to the loping 4/4 beat.

At the conclusion of the hymn, all remain standing. Rev. Sypho instructs the members to turn to the response reading, also found in the bulletin. The verses are from Luke 1.26-30:

> And in the sixth month the angel Gabriel was sent from God unto a city of Galilee, named Nazareth, to a virgin espoused to a man whose name was Joseph, of the house of David; and the virgin's name was Mary. And the angel came in unto her, and said, Hail, thou that art highly favoured, the Lord is with thee; blessed art thou among women. And when she saw him, she was troubled at his saying, and cast in her mind what manner of salutation this should be. And the angel said unto her, Fear not, Mary; for thou hast found favor with God.

We are in the liturgical season of Advent, celebrating the Annunciation in the first week. Salem does not follow the Protestant lectionary, or employ the liturgical titles of the church year. Yet the Black community has an indigenous liturgical season which originates out of its own experience and worship of God. One would have to augment the traditional Christian demarcation of the year with the recognition of such extra-seasonal events as "Mother's Day," "Pastor's Day," "Men's Day," among others which mark points of extreme importance in the life of the church. (N.B. The Emancipation Proclamation is *not* recognized formally in the canon of worship, an interesting omission in light of the extreme claims by modern Black theologians who contend that the church is shaped by the Exodus ethos.)

The lack of formal theological classification, however, does not indicate a lack of theological orientation. Unlike the Roman Catholic doctrine and celebration which depict Mary as a celestial deity, exalted, invoked, and implored in prayer as a mediatrix, the Afro-Christian tradition recognizes Mary as an ancestor and fellow sufferer in the travail of faith and responsibility before God. She is a sister, a mother and a woman who knew the work and pain of child-bearing, rearing, and the tragedy of childlessness.

The reading is short, an interlude before the culminating moment in the congregation's role. The prayer chant consists of a sung version of the Lord's Prayer, an indispensable part of all church services. The importance of the prayer here is not its verbal content as much as the physical manner in which it is recited. All members are instructed to hold hands with each other. The congregation knows this moment instinctively and hands move toward those of adjacent congregants without prompting. Even members at the ends of the pews are stretching into the aisles to reach others' hands. Whether members sing or recite this prayer, the gesture demands an act of commitment. The ending finds everyone's hands elevated as the organ and drums bring the chant to a crashing conclusion.

Returning to one's seat, one feels different about oneself and one's neighbor. The drawn out singing, along with the continuous standing and holding hands, has served to break down the sense of individuation which each of us–with the exception those who took part in the early morning devotional circle–possesses. The rhythm creates a sense of unity and personal involvement, of *Gemeinschaft.* As we sit, we are not only less mindful of ourselves, we feel more comfortable with one another, having breached some of our walls of self-containment.

Rev. Sypho stands at the pulpit: "Let the church say Amen!" The response punctuates the opening section of the congregational worship. Rev. Sypho makes a few announcements. The organ again provides a soft accompaniment for his words, which are intoned in a melodious, reverential voice, making the mundane affairs of church business sound like sacred articulation. The organ and style of elocution sustain the devotional mood recently created.

Sister Renita Goldor, head of the Social Services Ministry (only one facet of her extensive church commitments), comes forward in the white uniform of the Usher Board. She announces the availability of assistance for families faced with the hardship of utility payments and food shortages. She is followed by a woman who announces the Nursing Home Visitation Ministry and its dates. A member of the Welcome Committee proceeds to the microphone and reads Luke 2:10-11:

> And the angel said unto him, Fear not: for, behold, I bring you good tidings of great joy, which shall be to all people. For unto you is born this day in the City of David a Saviour, which is Christ the Lord.

The reading from Luke again sounds the seasonal acknowledgement of Advent, while establishing the tone and spirit in which the greeting, welcome, and formal recognition of visitors will take place. The woman then recites the greeting from memory, the same greeting which is made in season and out, reminding visitors that if they are without a saving relationship with Jesus Christ *and* without a church home, Salem invites them to experience *both* this Sunday. She acknowledges individually each visitor who has completed the visitor's information card, by reading aloud name, city of origin, church and pastor. Each visitor stands as the name is called. Once again, the organist creates a soothing, reflective atmosphere.

The ritual of hospitality is a recognition and negotiation of the boundaries between insider and outsider. The experience of "threshold," "entry," "insider/outsider" has profound implications for a people whose survival has always depended upon judging the extent to which they are welcome. Black Americans' history as outsiders and strangers is told and retold in hymns, slave spirituals, blues, tales, and jokes. These expressions contain the ethos of a displaced people whose intuition and sensibilities have been sharpened by the edges of rejection and rebuke.

Much of Black American life is consumed by the acts of discerning, encountering, struggling against, and surmounting impenetrable boundaries, and at times finding ways to move back and forth across hostile social demarcations. Rituals of hospitality therefore command attention to and sensitive evaluation of any kind of boundary existing between people. The finesse and delicacy with which this moment is tendered are subject to the scrutiny of both guest and host.

Members of the Welcome Committee perform a crucial function, for they make it possible for new visitors to experience the personal side of a very large church. This moment in the service is not superficially ceremonious. Though relatively brief, its concentrated intensity reveals an important face of the community's collective personality. If Salem ever receives the epithet of being a "dicty" or "uppity" church, it will have received the kiss of death. It could survive poor leadership or mediocre preaching, but never the ignominy of inhospitality toward the stranger.

While the conjunction between relationship and fellowship is couched in the context of an oft-repeated, seemingly mundane formula of hospitality, the greeting is theologically laden (and will receive closer analysis later in the paper). The Black church combines threads of evangelical theology which emphasize salvation through an exclusive encounter with Jesus, along with the Afro-Christian emphasis upon communal relationality as both liturgical context and mediation for the event of the encounter.

The standing visitors are asked to take their seats. The Welcome Committee member returns to her pew. The choir begins a mid-tempo number: "Worthy is the Lamb." The congregation begins to enter in, clapping in punctuated rhythm, bodies rocking side to side, following the choir. Soon the members make visible signs of participation, responding to the declarations of praise in the song:

> He died for you and me and everybody,
> He was slain for me and you, yes He was!
> He died that you and I might have life,
> He is the Lamb, praise His name.

(The bulletin devotes an entire page to the theme, "The Names of Our Lord")[3]

Pastor's Service

During the middle of this gospel selection, without fanfare or ceremonial announcement, the pastor enters. He is alone, without special vestment or iconographic jewelry. He strides down a side aisle and emerges into the pulpit while the congregation's attention is focused upon the choir and its energetic director, whose combined efforts have managed to bring a number of people to their feet, clapping, swaying.

Pastor Williams takes his seat between Rev. Sypho and Rev. Isaiah. Rev. Sypho, next in command to the pastor, dresses in a fashion slightly more flamboyant than that of the other ministers. In contrast, Rev. Isaiah wears subdued and darker colors like the deacon. Together these men symbolize two dimensions of the head pastor's office. Pastors in the Black church are still not only revered and esteemed by their flock, but are expected to deport themselves in a manner appropriate to the gravity of their calling. Pastors are people of communal and cosmic import, for they are not called by churches but by God. Pastors must be able to bear witness to a personal encounter with God, an undeniable moment of transformation which qualifies them for the office. On the other hand, Black pastors are also expected to represent the social aspirations and achievements of the church members. They are expected to be successful and to demonstrate the trappings of success.

Historically this has meant that Black pastors dressed the way that many members would have liked to be able to dress. Pastors drove cars which members could not afford. The members, however, could take pride in the fact that *their* pastor wore the finest clothes and drove the finest car, and in making these provisions for him, they too were elevated in the eyes of others. These values have endured across the generations, even though today's professional church member could certainly afford a car equal in value and status to the pastor's. Pastor Williams' distinction in this aspect of his role is not so much what he drives and wears, but the way he acquires it. Legends abound about his purchase of a late model Jaguar with cash, no time-payments or loans. Tailored suits and other fashionable items speak of a style highly admired throughout the entire Black community.

The other dimension of his pastoral role is fulfilled with equal effectiveness. For he not only represents the community's social aspirations, he embodies the consoling presence and power of God. This an important yet elusive point which must be disentangled from the classical, white Western tradition of understanding God and Jesus through Aristotelian philosophical terms of "virtues" and "attributes." Not that these conceptual approaches lack integrity or accuracy. They simply have little to do with African and Afro-American frames of reference for understanding God, even if this God is called by the same name and His son is known as Jesus. Pastor Williams' pastoral acumen is based not only on what phenomenologists of aesthetics call an "affecting presence," but also upon his powerful presentations, enactments and invocations of God's power.

His affecting presence has a dual dimension, for it is both visible and pervasive beyond the visible. While Pastor Williams is rarely seen about the church, his presence is felt throughout most if not all of its activities. Unlike pastors who mingle, mill about, attend fish fries, chicken suppers, softball games, and are immersed within their congregations, Pastor Williams is strangely absent, removed, often out of sight and out of town on executive business. Yet while absent, he remains strangely ubiquitous. This quality is powerfully illustrated by a response to a question I asked Rev. Isaiah. Rev. Isaiah had first heard of Pastor Williams while attending seminary in Ohio. He was able to experience Pastor Williams' preaching first hand, and heard tapes and saw videos of his services. In struggling to discern God's call upon his life, he felt led toward Atlanta. Before deciding to move from Ohio with his wife and family, he visited Salem's Wednesday night prayer service. His impressions and feelings about Pastor Williams were confirmed that evening, for he was deeply moved by the intensity and depth of prayer among Salem's members. He had often witnessed this depth and passion in the sermons and in the personality of Pastor Williams. The basis of his decision, however, rested upon the fact that Pastor Williams did not then, nor does he now, lead the prayer services. Rev. Isaiah was so moved to his decision by the manner in which Pastor Williams' presence had become part of the congregation in his absence.

Marsha Isaiah, Rev. Isaiah's wife, best summarized the visible dimension of Pastor Williams' affecting presence. I asked her how she felt during the moments before Pastor Williams arrives at the pulpit.

> I am full of anticipation. When he's there, as soon as I see him, I just feel better in church. But when I'm looking forward to seeing him—and I do every time—and then suddenly realize that he's not there and that somebody else is preaching that Sunday—and we've

had some good preachers, some excellent preachers when he's gone—when I find out he's not there, I just sink. It's not the same; it's just empty.

The fact that Pastor Williams' entrance is neither grand nor ceremonial testifies to the personal power of this man. While his entrance seemed to be a low-key event from my perspective, my conversation with Mrs. Isaiah and with others indicates that the pastor's solitary and seemingly casual arrival never goes unnoticed. From this moment, the services assume a different tenor. Pastor Williams' presence shapes the expectations of the congregation toward a different dimension of worship, and ultimately a different manifestation of God's power. (I will return to this distinction later.) For now it is important to note that the worship and the members have embarked upon a new trajectory with a new destination, in contrast to the telos of the early morning devotions.

The choir has elicited approving applause for its efforts. As the choir members take their seats, Pastor Williams steps into the pulpit to welcome the visitors to Salem. After the visitors are welcomed, the church literally welcomes itself. Under the pastor's direction, members are encouraged to stand, greet their neighbor, and then move out of the pews to welcome others (especially visitors) with the words, "God loves you and so do I." The orderly assembly suddenly disintegrates into a mass of omnidirectional movement. People are hugging each other in the aisles, ushers are parading up and down waving, men are extending vigorous Black handshakes, children are scurrying about. While I have been in numerous churches where this ritual of directed fellowship feels forced and strained, at Salem the preparations through the actions of the service preceding it have created a sufficient feeling of unity to make this moment comfortable. Although I did not register as a visitor or stand during the general invitation to unregistered visitors, I am repeatedly approached by congregants, both male and female, with affection and sincerity. While these are the signs of a healthy church body, the actions hold special meaning at this point in the service.

Both the devotional service and the joint singing by the choir and congregation have been ongoing attempts to break down the distance between members through collective action and through individual acts of reciprocal affirmation. In the devotional service, the affirmation rituals of the deacons and their powerful prayers and hymns, along with the commitment, openness and participation of the members, achieved this end. In the singing by choir and congregation, the leadership was shared between the choir director and Rev. Sypho, and thus was more varied in focus. The primary activity took place among the members themselves. Under the pastor's leadership, these efforts now continue. The pastor speaks over the music, selecting certain musical phrases, annotating the lyrics with his own commentary.

The pastor's entry into the middle of the service is quite different from the manner in which a Catholic priest leads the community in worship. The Catholic community is constituted by authority, declaration, the power of office. The Black community consists of enacted rather than formally declared relationality, since the pastor's ability to lead the congregation depends upon the people first *experiencing* themselves as a community; only then can the service move into other realms. The Catholic ritual which stresses in its theology the pre-existence of a "mysterious body" of Christ, one which is neither *Gemeinshaft* nor *Gesellschaft*, is enacted by the liturgy. With this theology, which builds the service around the actions performed upon various sacramental objects, it is possible to hold service with a congregation of one: the priest. Christ is sacramentally resident in the Eucharist placed in the mouth. In the Afro-Christian tradition, one must invoke the Spirit, interact, and receive the reality of the Spirit through the generative, creative labor of the self.

Pastor Williams intones: "Give God a hand clap" at the conclusion of the selection. He makes several comments, noting coming events in the church's celebration of Advent. The Lord's supper will be on the last Sunday of the year. A "watch night" service will be held with the sons of the church preaching. Pastor Williams then reads a letter from the Executive Office of President Bush, commending his "leadership and membership in a ministry to chemically-dependent individuals."

While these actions convey instruction and information, the tone and content also convey authority, power and prestige which the pastor commands and in which the church participates. The letter from the President recognizes the pastor's prominent standing. In the context of worship, these mundane moments give breadth and depth to the pastor's persona and power.

After establishing his place of prominence in the pulpit, the pastor introduces the first formal section of his part of the service, the Bible study. Today's lesson will examine Proverbs 3 and Nehemiah 5. While members locate their Bibles and turn to the appropriate pages, the Williams Inspirational Singers perform "I'm Glad, So Many Years." The selection praises Jesus in a spiritual, joyful yet serious tone. By the end of the musical selection, Bibles are open, pencils and note pads in hand. The church is ready to receive the pastor's well-prepared and carefully crafted lessons.

Pastor Williams has amended the typical traditional Baptist worship with the introduction of formal Bible lessons within the context of worship. On one hand, this innovation is an adoption of styles which became popular in many new churches and "televangelist" ministries, attracting not only well-educated members but those who hunger for carefully wrought instruction. Williams is a formidable teacher as well as preacher, and his lessons at times sound like sermons. Nevertheless, the lessons maintain their structure which makes his presentations accessible to all and meaningful both to the well educated and less educated members of his church.

Like Salem's other liturgical adaptations, the Bible lessons have been shaped according to Black cultural norms. Williams' teaching is a model in Black pulpit poetic pedagogy. Many teachers could learn from his style. He announces the Biblical passages again, now adding verse numbers to the chapter in Proverbs (3.7-10).

> Be not wise in thine own eyes: fear the Lord and depart from evil. It shall be health to thy navel and marrow to thy bones. Honor the Lord with thy substance, and with the first fruits of all thine increase: so shall thy barns be filled with plenty, and thy presses shall burst out with new wine.

The chapter and verse numbers also appear in the bulletin with page numbers referring to Salem's house Bible. At every level, the members' sense of participation in a shared activity within a community is reinforced. Pastor Williams now implores the congregation:

> I want your commitment to remain after I preach the sermon, to keep the order and the structure that we now have. We'll lift our tithes and offerings at that time, then afterwards I'll privilege those who want to leave. Please do that for us.

His instruction can be understood as an attempt to hold his congregation's attention for the completion of the entire service, emphasizing each part as important and deserving of the members' full participation. The instruction could also be interpreted as a strategy to achieve the maximum contribution from the gathered body. The collection of the tithes and offerings usually precedes the Bible lesson. Announcing from the pulpit its relocation not only indicates the liturgy's flexible structure, open to improvisation, but also signals the purpose of the day's sermon. The theme of the lesson and sermon addresses the question of resources: those of God, the church, and individual believers. Pastor Williams, as we shall see, is rearranging the order of the service so that the structure will support and embody his message, and strengthen the members' commitment to his articulation of the church's mission.

Pastor Williams' lessons, masterfully expounded, will be examined below. Lesson content is important for the members' expectations and assessment of the lessons, as evidenced by the number who take notes. For his part, Pastor Williams is careful to create an atmosphere conducive to learning. His sentences are delivered in a deliberate cadence, which moves slowly but with a variable rhythm, punctuating important points with extended pauses and accents. The timbre of his full-throated baritone creates a mellifluous atmospheric current. His voice is a finely tuned musical-elocutionary instrument capable of chromatic modulations and tonal variations ranging from husky guttural "whoops" to high-pitched screams. While the full range of his acoustic spectrum is reserved for the sermon, the Bible lesson offers introductory exposure to his vocal possibilities.

I know, brothers and sisters, that whenever I begin to talk about finances that I am talking about something that is very, very, very relevant to everybody under the sound of my voice. Someone has said on occasion, and rightfully so, that the most sensitive nerve in the human body is that nerve that runs from the heart to the pocketbook. My brothers and my sisters, God has a plan for you. And God's plan for you is that you will not die in bondage. His plan for you is that you will have liberty, that you will have freedom. God does not want His children to be in bondage to anything or anybody but to our Lord and Savior, Jesus Christ.

When you are in bondage to Lord Jesus Christ, that is perfect liberty, that is freedom at its best. The Bible says, "He that my Son sets free is free indeed." Now an illustration to our text today is found in Nehemiah, chapter 5. Nehemiah becomes an illustration of what we are talking about.

The people in the day when Nehemiah lived were in the midst of a building program, just like we are about to embark upon. They were building, re-building the wall that had been torn down which went round and about the city of Jerusalem. And it was God's will, and it was God's work for them, for God had ordered it done. And you know I believe with all my soul that whatever God orders somebody, God pays for. God wanted it done, so God enabled it to be done.

The acquisition of this property over on Center Hill, which had been so impossible to acquire and possess, God wanted it done. [Oh yes] Church, I believe that He wants us to expand and build something now for the people. Therefore I am claiming that God is going to enable us to do what it is He has led us to do. [Yes Lord, Amen]

And I want you to keep in mind, now, that anytime God says, "Let us rise, get up and build," simultaneously–at the same moment–the Devil says to all of his imps, "Rise, get up, and stop him." [Alright] And that's what he tried to do in Nehemiah's day, and that's the way he tried to stop them, to bring them into financial bondage. 'Cause if the people were in financial bondage, they could not do what God wanted them to do.

Now the same Devil that tried to put these people in financial bondage the Devil who is going to try to put us in financial bondage. If you are a member of this church, and you are in financial bondage, we'll not be able to do what God wants us to do, 'cause we have gotten out of His will and into financial bondage. So with that in mind, let us look at the scripture, Nehemiah 5, and I am reading verse 1 through 5.

Pastor Williams introduces the scripture story by creating a unitary frame of reference for the members. He accomplishes the task in three movements. First, he identifies and addresses a vital subject. Even though many of Salem's members are middle class, significant segments belong to the working class and lower economic strata. But even the solidly middle class members dwell on the precipice of financial insecurity. The new Black middle class invests a higher percentage of income in disposable consumer items and services than the national norm. Black consumers make less, save less and spend more than their white counterparts. Working within institutions that traditionally excluded them, Black employees face the perils of low seniority and high visibility, a profile under assault in this era of aggressive affirmative action regression. Commanding the attention of his membership, Pastor Williams has entered a realm fraught with anxiety and insecurity. Secondly, the pastor is reading the Nehemiah text in light of Salem's undertaking to acquire and develop land for the construction of a retirement home for the elderly. Thirdly, he is also reading Salem's mission in light of the Nehemiah text, giving both events the same structure and single frame within the activity of God. The Biblical narrative is part of Salem's events, and Salem's story is part of Biblical events.

Many of the members are prepared for this moment through Wednesday evening's prayer meeting, whose prayers and testimonies were shaped around struggle and divine resourcefulness. In addressing one of the deepest needs of individual members, Pastor Williams also articulates and focuses upon the needs of the church.

[Reads Nehemiah 5:1-5]: "And there was a great cry of the people and of their wives against their brethren the Jews. For there were that said, We, our sons, and our daughters, are many: therefore take up corn for them, that we may eat, and live. Some also there were that said, We have mortgaged our lands, vineyards, and houses, that we might buy corn, because of the dearth.   There were also that said, We have borrowed money for the king's tribute, and that upon our lands and vineyards. Yet now our flesh is as the flesh of our brethren, our children as their children: and lo, we bring into bondage our sons and our daughters to be servants, and some of our daughters are brought unto bondage already: neither is it in our power to redeem them; for other men have our lands and vineyards."

How sad, how pitiful, what a tragedy all of this is, because the people of God in this passage were in *financial bondage*. Let us look at what trou-bles they were having and see if it reminds us of anything going on in our own lives.

Pastor Williams is instructing what amounts to a 2,000-member student body. The teaching occasion, however, does not transform the sanctuary into a classroom; rather the setting and morning-long activities have transformed instruction into worship. While Pastor Williams verbally instructs, he includes the necessary cues, which keep the members' attention focussed upon the text and the lesson (by iterating the theme of the tithe in his summing statement after reading the passage in Nehemiah, and by repeating the verse and chapter numbers). His presence and persona also command, shape and evoke a reverential focus on and reception of the lesson.   His magisterial presence combined with his verbal capacity to relate the text to the existential condition of the congregation–to make the Word of God and the lives of God's people a single story–infuse the pedagogical moment with liturgical energy.

The generation of this energy of worship is not, as we have seen, solely the pastor's work, but is also the people's work.   (The etymology of the word "liturgy" is "work of the people.") Much of the morning's work has been spent engendering the conditions and experiences that will enable the members to become a unified people for this moment. And much has been done without the pastor.   At this point, the pastor's task is to probe and explore the affective realm of his congregants who harbor multiple layers of anxiety as a result of living in a condition of financial insecurity. In so doing, Pastor Williams enables the members to become as fully present to one another in the committed act of worship as his persona is to them–or to be wholly present before God.

[Pastor Williams continues]: Look at verse 1. Verse 1 of Chapter 5 of Nehemiah says: "And there was a great cry of the people and of their wives against their brethren the Jews."

You see, there was *strife*, that's what it's saying, because they were fighting, arguing and squabbling over money. And may I ask, did *your* family ever argue, fight, fuss, cuss, squabble over money? Have you ever known of a church to divide itself because of money? Ha! [chuckles] Don't look so holy this morning! [Alright! stirs of laughter, affirmations of the pastor's accuracy]

In marriage ceremonies, there's a part that the priest or preacher says in binding two people in the holy bonds of matrimony. A segment of that ceremony which says, "Till *death* do us part." But looking at our situation now, perhaps it should say, "Till *debt* do us part."

If we trust Marshal McLuhan's insight that every joke masks a grievance, the congregation's uncomfortable laughter in response to the pastor's depiction of marital conflict around financial issues is confirmation of the accuracy of his probe.

So then there was strife among the brethren. But not only was there strife, we see also in the days of Nehemiah a shortage of human needs in verse 2. For there were those that said, "We, our sons, and our daughters, are many; therefore we take up corn for them, so that we may *eat* and *live*." That meant that there were some of them that were literally on *welfare*. [Oh God (Deacon Napper)] People were so bad off that they had to have offerings taken up for them, for the people were struggling and suffering, just to make ends meet. They were having a tough time surviving, just trying to live on the bare means of life. [Oh yes] So there's the second thing we see happening in the days of Nehemiah: shortages of human need.

Pastor Williams has entered another region which is resonant with painful overtones for his congregants. While Salem is a middle class church in appearance and style, there are members who are forced to rely upon the resources of the state's welfare system. But the issue's delicacy stretches beyond the roster of members, for many of Salem's congregants who are self-sustaining participants in the labor force are nonetheless related to families who are economically dependent. This situation places both the self-supporting and the state-dependent workers in a tension-wrought position in relation to one another and to the values implicit in Pastor Williams' interpretation of verse 2. This tension will be more fully explored in the commentary below; here it is important to note that the pastor is taking delicate steps upon a tender path toward a conflicted region in the relationships, attitudes and values of the members.

And then thirdly, they have mortgaged their houses and their land. You see that in verse 3 [recites verse 3]. Now they weren't mortgaging their house so that they could build luxurious swimming pools. They weren't mortgaging their vineyards and land just so they could add an extra bedroom. But they were mortgaging their farms, vineyards and land so that they could merely get the daily necessities of life. [Pray hard, Salem] Just so they could have food that they could then put on their table.

Pastor Williams sentences are filled with heterogeneous borrowings of nouns from two separate and distinct cultural and chronological realms. "Vineyards" and "land" belong to the Biblical depiction of Hebrew religion set in 445 BCE Palestine, while "swimming pool" and "extra bedroom" belong to the world of his listeners. Placing the two opposing chronological realms together in a single sentence creates a new realm. The semantic anachronism stitches two dimensions into a seamless world of time.

And then as we read further we also see that they were in all kinds of debt. Debt was on them in every shape, every form, any fashion that was imaginable. [recites verse 4] That means they were borrowing money, not to make an investment; they were borrowing money so as to pay their taxes. And when it says, "king's tribute," that's another way of saying paying their income tax. Have you ever borrowed money, brothers and sisters, so as to pay your income tax? Ha! That's what they were doing. They borrowed money which was the king's tribute, meaning to pay their taxes [Oh yeah! (Deacon Napper)], and this was a time of high taxation.

Taxes were forever always around, taxes will always get you down.

Jesus said, when He was here: "The poor shall be with you always...." [Oh yeah! (Deacon Napper)] May I add to that this morning: "Taxes will be with you always." [stirring response: Have mercy, that's right] Because of all these things...and these people found themselves in financial bondage.

Pastor Williams' rhyming couplets ("around/down") and humorous substitutions placed in the mouth of Jesus not only add emphasis to his lesson but provide the congregation an opportunity to affirm the pastor's rhetorical prowess.

Look again now, in verse 5, and you'll see it again. [recites verse 5] What he is saying here is that we have mortgaged not only our houses–we have mortgaged not only our lands and vineyards–we have also mortgaged the future of our children. And when you think about it, that's the way it is with us today. These days in which we now live, this is the first time in American history when our children will not be able know that their day will not be better than their parents' day. We who are living now are enjoying things that our parents and foreparents could not enjoy. But with the way the world is being set up, with more than $200 billion in deficit spending, it means that our children's and our children's children's future has been mortgaged by *our* indebtedness. And so that when our children come into this world, they will not be born with a *legacy* at their disposal, but instead they will have a *load*, for there is going to be debt hanging over their shoulders. They were sold in slavery, they were sold as slaves and servants, and it doesn't say here, it doesn't sound very good about the people in Nehemiah's day–but they were bogged down because they were in what I call *financial bondage*.

Pastor Williams has accomplished a variety of tasks within the first section of the Bible lesson. His approach to expanding upon the text relies heavily upon an African/Black American stylistic technique of rhythmically repeating a simple theme while making elaborate variations, only to return to the repeated phrase. This pattern can also be identified visually in African fabric and ornamental designs. One also hears this pattern in jazz, known as the riff.

Repetition here not only articulates the lesson's theme, but also unifies the Biblical situation of Nehemiah's predicament with the predicament of Salem's members. As mentioned above, Pastor Williams relies upon anachronistic interlacings within the sentence; the situational logic leads to the inescapable conclusion of an identical dilemma. Achieving situational singularity is not, however, the re- sponsibility of the pastor alone. The congregation has affirmed, at many points throughout the lesson, the accuracy of his depiction of their situation's exigencies. His accurate probing evokes affective responses which begin to create a new situation, a lived and invested moment within the environment of worship. This new situation is the creation and the work of worship, and therefore requires the participation and involvement of all those who are present. Consequently, the next movement in the lesson directly addresses the members. The logic is inherent in the performance: first, evocation of a unitary situation by making the Biblical and contemporary conditions one, then a direct address of the new situation which is now present. This second movement is an exploration of the members' experiences, which they have made present.

Now I want to know are you in *financial* bondage, and I want to give you a little test so you can find out and make a determination on your own. You shouldn't answer these questions out loud; just to yourselves, nobody should know but you, and of course God. Here's the test...

Do you find yourself charging daily expenditures, charging them because you don't have the cash to pay for them? What I say daily expenditures, I'm talking about necessities like your prescriptions being filled, your drugs, do you have to charge your gasoline to go in your car, the groceries to go on your table? Not that you charge them so that you can keep an expense account, not for that reason or that you don't like to carry a lot of cash around, but do you find yourself using plastic money because you don't have the real thing to buy your daily necessities? Do you put off paying bills that are due this month and say you are going to pay them next month? Do you? Do you find yourself borrowing money so that you can pay expenses like your insurances, your house payment, your rent, your taxes, to pay your regular expenses that are coming due? Do you find yourself having to borrow money in order that you can do that?

Do you really know—next question—do you really, really know how much money you owe, I mean really know? Or are you afraid to look? [widespread laughter] [Oh Lord! (Deacon Napper); people raise their hands] I mean have you sat down and totaled up *all* of your bills? Gotten to the point that you can literally say, "Well, we owe this, so we've got to have this amount of money this week to pay these bills; next week we got to have this amount of money to pay *those* bills"—or whatever. A lot of people are afraid to do that, and they literally don't do that, and consequently they have no idea of knowing who it is they owe, and therefore they know not how much they owe. [Amen! (Deacon Napper)]

Let me ask you another question: Do you have collectors, creditors writing you nasty letters, calling you on the telephone, disturbing your employer on the job, threatening to garnishee your job? Have you been borrowing new loans, so that you could pay off old loans? [Oh God! (Deacon Napper)] Um-hmm... One other question now...

Don't answer this one now: Do you and your wife, or do you and your husband argue about money? Hmmmm...Get this one... Theirs was a perfect marriage except for one feminine flaw, He was quick on the deposit, but she was faster on the draw. [extended laughter by entire congregation]

Do you and your spouse ever have misunderstandings about money? Have you ever considered the idea about being dishonest about money? You know, trying to get out of paying your rent, going to shave a corner on your taxes. You know... strike a deal, you know it's not right, you know it's not straight. You're tempted somehow to do something dishonest? Do you?

Do you, every Lord's Day, bring 10% of your income plus for the work of God through the church? Do you? On God's Day, bring

God's tithe so that God's work might be done God's way? Or do you say...[in character]: "I can't afford to tithe. The church doesn't need it. I need it better than they need it. I need it more than anybody else over there need it."

Somehow you just rationalize and rationalize that you are really obeying God because you got to take care of yourself first. "Plus I give to the United Way," "I give to the United Negro College Fund," "I give to the Cancer Society." Anytime you hear anybody justifying *not* giving to God's house because they give to charitable organizations, 99.9% of the time–they're lying. So you have failed to honor God with your tithes on God's day.

Now if these things which I have just asked you are true, if one of them is true, especially if two or three are true, and doubly specially if just about all of them are true, my friend, my sister, my brother, you are in financial bondage and the Devil has you right under his thumb. Why? Because if he stops you, keeps you bound, then that means the church is bound–because you, we, us, all of us *are* the church. So when you are in financial bondage, the church is in financial bondage, and the work of God cannot be done.

Now you say [in character]: "Well, this sermon is certainly not for me, preacher, because, well, I have plenty. I have a bank account and it's full, and it's stayin' that way. You talking to the poor folks, you not talking 'bout me. I'm not worried 'bout anything. Man–one thing about me–I'm not in no financial bind."

But you see, you could be in bigger bondage than the poor people are and not realize it. Because whether you know it or not, the rich people can be in bondage just as well as the poor. Some of you who are rich may be slaves to your money, just as the poor people are. Look with me in Nehemiah chapter 5, and look down at verse 6 and see what I'm talking about: "And I was very angry when I heard their cry and heard these words." In other words, Nehemiah is saying, "It grieved me when I saw that God's people were in bondage. It not only grieved me, it made me become righteously indignant."

[verse 7]: "Then I consulted with myself, and I rebuked the nobles, and the rulers, and said unto them, Ye exact usury, every one of his brother. And I set a great assembly against them."

Who were the rulers, who were the nobles? These were the wealthy people who were shrewd. And what was done... they had been taken advantage of in that situation. You see, they knew the poor people were defenseless, and they knew that they had the power of manipulation and interest–so they wanted to *rob* from the poor

people, and make themselves richer and richer and richer.   In other
words, they were putting God's people in financial bondage.

The theme of the lesson, and the reference to the congregation,
allows the pastor to intertwine, interweave or "textualize" his material.
These are all spatial, linear, representational metaphors for
comprehending the process of stitching several forms–dramatic
dialogue, Biblical text, proverb, allegory–into one presentation.   But
the oral mode is *presence*, not representation.   It does not exist in
some prior mode or realm, waiting to be *re*-presented.   The oral mode
comes into existence, now at hand, in the present moment, before and
with the congregation.

They [the nobles] were acquiring their land, they were acquiring their
wealth, they were acquiring all that they wanted to possess. Nothing
is wrong with acquiring land, nothing is wrong with acquiring
wealth, for it is God who gives you the power to get wealthy.   But
what happens is that, in this text, the people were extorting, they were
conniving and using unethical methods of getting money. They were
getting fat, so that the rich people, the well-off people, in Nehemiah's
day were *tricking* [reference to whoring], and pulling all kinds of
tricks–in reality, they too were in...financial bondage.

Let me ask you a question to find out if you are in financial bondage.
Those of you who are well off...those of you who have got... Do you
find yourself having more faith in your money than you have in
God? Hmmm...do you?

When you pray do you ask God to give you your daily bread
everyday? You don't do that 'cause you got plenty? Then you're
trusting in your money. And I want to tell you, one day your money
is going to fail you.

Do you find yourself trusting in things more than you trust in God?
Hmmm?
Do you wear your clothes or do your clothes wear you? [mmm, that's
right]
Do you spend your money or does your money spend you?
[congregational murmurs in response]
Are your personal goals for life no longer God's goals, but have they
become your goals? If so, then you are in bondage.

One more question. Is every penny of that wealth that you have,
available to God? Not one tenth, but 100% of the wealth you have.
Down to that last half-cent. Is it available to God? I mean have you
said, "God, You can have it all. It's all Yours, the shirt off my back,
it's Yours." I'm saying God's going to ask you for the shirt off your

back. But if it was you knowing that God was asking–no preacher was involved, no organization was involved–but God was asking [Oh yeah (Deacon Napper)], is it available, all of it, is it all available to Him? [Oh yeah Salem]

"Take my silver and gold
Not one mite will I withhold..."
Yet I'm holding with *all-l-l* my might.

Brothers and sisters, if you have not committed yourself to Him totally, you are in bondage; it's not yours. You are a steward over it. God is the owner of it, and God has the right to demand, anytime, upon that which is His. [Well Salem (Deacon Napper)] He has a right to do that because you do not own it. You are merely a steward.

Do you have it, or does it have you? Do you have a burning desire to get more money? Now God gives some people the ability to make money, but if *that's* the thing that melts your butter, making money is what motivates you, then you are in bad shape. You're bound, you're in bondage. I don't care how many suits you have in your wardrobe, you can't wear but one at a time. It makes no difference how many rooms you have in your house, you can't sleep in but one at a time. You just want more! and more! and more! and more! And the more you get, the more you want. Haven't you found yet [begins to shout] that things no matter how many of them you get, and how much of it is, [shouts] things will not satisfy!!! [Oh Lord]

Why? I'll tell you why. There's a little thing in every heart and it's called eternity, and eternity cannot be satisfied with the things of this world. So Mr. Rich Man, are you making money and you ought to be praying? Are you making money and you ought to be thanking God? If you are, then you are in bondage. [Oh Lord (Deacon Napper)]

Mr. Business Man, do you find yourself cutting a deal, shaving a point here and trying to do something that's totally unethical? If so, then you are in financial bondage. Taking advantage of somebody else puts you in financial bondage. Now God does not want people, whether they be rich or poor, to be financially bound.

Now I want to give you, this morning, six principles, and to me they are marvelous principles indeed, that if you were to take heed today, you would come out of your financially-bound stupor. The principles are just as true as I'm standing here, speaking to you today. The first is what I call the principle of priority. [Alliteration assists the memory, and makes the term poetically pleasing.] Nehemiah is an example of what we are preaching about. Look at verse 14 of the fifth chapter. Verse 14 says:

"Moreover from the time that I was appointed to be their governor in the land of Judah, from the twentieth year even unto the two and thirtieth year of Artaxerxes the king, that is, twelve years, I and my brethren have not eaten the bread of the governor."

What he is saying is that I haven't taken any salary I was due. I was supposed to be paid, but I haven't received any salary. I have not lived off the government as if it was mine. That's what he's saying.

[verse 15] "But the former governors that had been before me were chargeable unto the people, and had taken of them bread and wine, besides forty shekels of silver; yea, even their servants bare rule over the people: but so did not I, because of the fear of God."

Notice that the last part of verse 15 says, "but so did not I." Why, why is it that I didn't do that "because of the *fear* of God?" What that means is that there is something that controls my life, there is something that does not cause me to take advantage of a situation I'm in. You see Nehemiah had the ability to get fat if he wanted to. He could have lived the soft life. He could have had his hand in the public till. But he didn't do it. "I didn't do that because of the fear of God."

When he said he "feared God," he was saying, "I honored God, I believed in God, I respected God, in other words, God was first...in...my...life!! So God is priority in my life and whatever I do...I do...because...of God!!"

The first principle, the first principle to financial freedom...you must prioritize your life!!! Priority: Get God in His rightful place!!! Huh? Where is it? Where is God's rightful place? [Matthew 6:33]: "Seek ye *first* the kingdom of God and His righteousness; and all these *things* shall be added unto you."

Listen, brothers and sisters, if you put things first and God second, don't care what you got, you start out a failure. And if you put God first and things second, then God will take care of the *things*. Let me show you what I'm talking about, let me give you some scriptures on that, some background. This is what Proverbs 3:9-10 is talking about: "Honor the Lord with all thy substance, and the first fruits of all thine increase: so shall the barns be filled with plenty, and thy presses shall burst out with new wine." So then God is not going to take second place to anybody or anything, and not until you let God in first place will you have absolute right [sic] to expect God to give you financial freedom. Why should God free you of all your financial indebtedness, why should God free you of your financial bondage if He's not going to be first in your life? Do you want to be financially free? Do you think God is going to let you be financially free so God will let you run around big, and fat, and sloppy...drinking and eating up everything and don't have Him in His rightful place?

Brothers and sisters, our job is: we are to love people, use things, and worship God. Most of us worship money, love things, and use people. [widespread laughter and affirming responses] One question: [shouting] *Is God first in your life?* That's *not* a rhetorical question I'm asking you. Ask yourself the question, ask it down in the precincts of your soul, "Is God first?" As you sit here, is God in absolute total control, first in your life, Lord of your life? Is Jesus Christ Lord of all? "Seek ye first the kingdom of God."

So Nehemiah had priority in his life. "I live this way. [shouting] I do it because there is a divine priority. It is my fear of God." And fear of God, the Bible says, is the beginning of wisdom. [voice rising] Fear of the Lord [Praise God (Deacon Napper)] is also the beginning of having true wealth. So Principle One of coming out of financial bondage is that I prioritize my life to the point that God is given his rightful place, and that is first place.

Principle Two... The second principle is called the principle of industry. Industry! The word "industry" simply means work. Work. Look at verse 16 of Nehemiah, chapter 5: "Yea, also I continued in the work of this wall, neither bought we any land: and all my servants were gathered thither unto the work."

Nehemiah was the governor of the people. He didn't have to work. He could have gotten out of work if he wanted to. He made up his mind that he was going to work, for here's a principle of financial freedom. And it is spelled W-O-R-K, work!! Let me tell you something about human nature. Do you know why most people want to make more money? The only reason is that they want the time to come so that they can sit down and they won't have to work. [Yes sir; yes pastor, yes; that's right; Lord, yes] A lot of people have the idea—"boy, if I just had enough money I wouldn't have to work." All they want to do is sit down! [shouting] Sit down! "I'll be so glad when this day is over, I'm going to sit down! I can't wait to get home so I can pull off my shoes and [shouting] sit down!" [widespread congregational response, humorous and affirming] "The weekend can't come fast enough for me to get...ooohhh, I wish today was Friday so I could go home and sit down."

These sections are dramatic illustrations, verbal and gestural enactments of slothful behavior which will only lead to ruin. The pastor is satirizing sensibilities and values both within his congregation and the larger community.

That's what's wrong with us now [shouting]. We can't get nowhere, we ain't got nothing, ain't trying to get nothing, all because the little bit we got, we ain't doing nothing but just..."sit down"!!! [Oh yeah, have mercy Lord] "A few years from now, I'm going to retire from my job, and I can't wait, so I can retire and go sit down!!" And you know, we've carried this idea of sitting down on over to glory. We got that ol' song, "When I get to heaven, I'm going to put on my long white robe."

So you don't think it's me, lick your fingers now, get into this sermon with me, go to Proverbs 20:4. Lick your fingers now, come on... "The sluggard shall not...

The sluggard shall not...
The sluggard shall not...
The sluggard shall not...have nothing." [Lord have mercy]

In other words, the sluggard, when the frosty morning comes, the old sluggard wakes up [yawns comically]. The alarm clock goes off, and the old sluggard peeps out and sees the fields got to be plowed, but all that frost is on the window pane, and it feels so good under the covers. "Man, I'm not going out there today," so he pul-l-ls the covers up to his chin, and [snores loudly] sleeps, goes back to sleep. Now, he's not going to prosper. And he's not prospering because God hadn't heard his prayers. You can't put it on God. He the one laying up on his behind, sleeping, won't get up, won't do nothing, then talk about God "ain't heard my prayers." Not because God caused him to fail—he's lazy. Therefore God will not bless him. "Sluggard" means "lazy bones."

The address is to the interior of the community and the individual's responsibility in relationship to God. The external forces of oppression, which take the form of unjust economic, social and political structures—the preoccupation of Latin and Black American theologians—are conspicuously absent. This is teaching from the Book of Wisdom, *not* Exodus.

Look down at Proverbs 20:13. "Love not sleep." In other words, wake up! "Love not sleep lest thou come to poverty." In other words, you going to sleep yourself broke. "That's alright, I ain't got nothing." That's why you ain't got nothing, you been sleeping too much.

Come on, lick, lick lick. Turn to Proverbs 28:19. Now remember, the writer of the Book of Proverbs is writing to the farmer, always remember that. "He that tilleth his land shall have plenty of bread." There is no substitute for work. We pray, "Give us this day our daily bread." Fine, but it also says, "If a man does not work, neither shall he eat" [II Thessalonians 3:10].

A lot of folk think "work is a dirty word." You look at some people and you say "work" and they think you cussin' them out. But let me tell you something, in the society we're in, the biggest drain in our society comes from people who won't work. Let me show you what I'm talking about: criminals, forgers [begins to shout], gamblers, pick-pockets, tramps, dope pushers, pimps, whores, prostitutes. You ain't got to say "Amen," I know I'm preaching to you!! [applause] And they cost us literally billions of dollars. Honest people, hardworking people, people who want to have something in life, people who want something for themselves...we're having to bear the burden of those who do not want [pause] to work!

Listen, Chesterfield said, "Idleness is the fool's holiday." John Bunyan said, "An idle brain is the devil's workshop." Have you ever noticed how when you don't have anything to do, you start thinking about, "yeah, you know, ha ha, yeah, um-hmmmm..." Hollins said, "An idle man is outside of the plans of God." Henry Ward Beecher said, "If we are idle, we are on the road to ruin."

This faith and prosperity theme is extremely popular today, now that every social stratum of North American Christendom has been able to reconcile the tensions between the self-indulgent principality of affluence and the demands of the Kingdom. The popularity once commanded by Jim Bakker and his wife, Tammy Fae, along with Rev. Jimmy Swaggart, both ministers in the Assembly of God denomination (whose rank and file members at one time came largely from the lower economic and social strata), was in part due to their ability to reassure their followers that their newly acquired middle-class consumer materialism was truly provided by God. All those *things* which used to be considered sinful such as television, movies, multiple cars, vacations, pagan theme parks such as Disneyland, carnivals–were also unaffordable.

But if one compares Pastor Williams' teaching on prosperity to its white counterpart, the difference is evident. Kenneth Copeland, J & T, Oral Roberts all stressed financial contributions and "hyper-faith" as the keystones to prosperity. Faith, defined by them as the defiance of reality, combined with Biblical literalism and steep percentages of one's gross income, were promised to multiply the believers' prosperity by hundred-folds.

The emphasis of Pastor Williams' teaching is self-discipline, delayed gratification, hard work, sacrifice, and responsibility–values which have become identified with conventional middle-class standards. But upon closer inspection, these values grow out of the tradition of cultivating Christian virtue. This tradition shaped both classical Western Christianity and African-American Christianity. One simply needs to refer to Booker T. Washington's autobiography, or that of Frederick Douglass, to find them replete with references that connect character, morality, faith and prosperity. Moral character, the quality of one's public behavior, is still assessed within the Black community in terms that go beyond the purely economic.

God said, "In the sweat of thy face thou shalt eat bread." Our government, since Reagan has moved out of the White House and hopefully Reaganomics with him, is trying to loosen up its belts to hand down more money to governmental agencies; they are giving more to welfare, more to Medicare, more to food stamps and housing. Brothers and sisters, let me tell you, welfare doesn't build character, Medicare and food stamps don't build character. Nothing builds character but WORK!!

[high, childlike, whining voice]: "Well, what about those who can't help themselves, Jasper?" I ain't talking about them! "Shouldn't you be taking care of them?" Yeah, you ought to be taken care of, of course you should, if you can't help yourself. But you shouldn't scream and lay up on the government and try to get the government to send you checks. Then there you are giving it to the man, and he got your check, and he not going to see you no more till the first of the month, then he come down and get in the bed with you and take your check again!! [The description of the familiar scenario stirs the church into animated response: Tell the truth, Reverend; you right today; Lord have mercy.]

Seldom do doctors agree about anything, but here is a prescription which has been recommended and unanimously accepted:
If your health threatens you, work...
If disappointment comes, work...
If you are rich, continue to work...
If your faith falters and your reason fails, work...
If your dreams are shattered and your hope is dead, work...
[mocking tone]:
$10,000 for an automobile
$8,000 for a piece of sod
$1,000 for my TV set, but
  a dollar I gave to God.
$50 for my fishing trip,
$15 for a rod,
$10 for the bait I use, but
  a dollar I gave to God.
Oh I have my church

and attend it some,
and I often nod,
  but I sit up straight and smile
  when I give my dollar to God.
The Bible teaches salvation is free
and the way of the transgressor is hard.
Since salvation is free, a dollar ought
  to be enough for Gawd.
But when it comes time for us to die
and I stand before my Lord,
will I be satisfied in my heart
  that a dollar was enough for God?

Principle four is reliability. God is reliable. Nehemiah reminded God that he had been faithful, and needed God to be reliable for him.

Principle five is integrity. Be about something, think well of your-self, be about something. It hurts me when I get off the plane, five white men run to the man–I'm there first, they take care of the white man first, 'cause I'm Black–because he figures I have no integrity–I'm not about anything–because my people are that way.

Principle six is sufficiency. Doesn't matter if Republican or Democrat wins. Doesn't matter if inflation jumps 15 points, if interest rates are 21% points. God is able to take care of His children. Do you think God's got to read the *Wall Street Journal* before He can take care of you? Do you think God's got to see what the Dow-Jones index is before He can take care of you? No, God will take care.

You're going to have to give all these principles achievement. God must be first. I guess what I'm saying in essence, brothers and sisters, as I leave you, is that you got to put Him first. God must be first. [end of teaching; sermon will begin below]

Black people do not separate justice from virtue. Clarence Thomas is thus an ambiguous character for the Black community. Since 54% of the Black community supported and 52% opposed him, the perplexity generated by this figure is evident, for he embodies the contradictions of the split realms of God's reality which white society has long relinquished its efforts to integrate: Leviticus and Exodus, wisdom and justice, personal responsibility and collective responsibility. These splits have become institutionalized and desecularized in white society, as can be seen in the values embraced by liberal vs. conservative political parties and churches.
Conservative theology stresses the primary variable of individual initiative, hard work, responsibility, in other words, personal, private morality as the key to addressing social ills of poverty and inequality.

In this view, the institutional, structural and corporate reality of injustice–especially its economic manifestations–has no ultimate responsibility in the individual's failures or plight. Liberal theology, on the other hand, stresses the bondage of the individual entangled in institutional, structural, and corporate machinations. Liberation is defined as challenging and changing this order.

Clarence Thomas is only the latest example of an increasing number of Black individuals who have become willing hosts to the psychological and ideological afflictions and contradictions, which characterize the modern West. Feminists call it "white men's disease," the malaise of the fractured, de-contextualized individual who exists and acts in disregard of the complex relational dimensions of his life and identity.

Relational perspectives have always informed the religious consciousness of traditional African-American Christians. Communities such as Salem and other church bodies that are heir to African-American traditional Christianity, which continues to cultivate a sense of relational identity, are rooted in the personal, communal and corporate realities of human existence. All of these dimensions, together, create a cosmos. The Black Christian cosmos, as Sorbel documents, reaches inward to the interior depths of the individual and outward to the transcendent realm of the eternal creator of the universe. But this cosmos, this comprehensive order is created not by symbolic objects but through enactments and embodied words. The emphasis is upon the kinetic creation and interactive, reciprocal enfleshment of human utterance. Therefore dramatic rather than noetic ritual predominates within these circles of worship. Even when the word is read, the reading moves toward drama rather than contemplation.

[Sermon begins]: One day Jesus was in the land of Galicia, and came upon the Lake of Gennesaret. There were two boats anchored there at harbor. Jesus stepped into one of these boats. It so happened that the boat he stepped in belonged to a fisherman named Simon. I heard him say, "Mister, this is my boat that you're in." Jesus said to him, "Uh, how is the fishing business?" The man said, "Well, sir, we been fishing all night but we have not caught anything." Jesus said, "Well, what I wish you'd let me do is use this boat, for the multitudes will be here in a moment, and I need to be able to launch it out in the water." [I'm doing alright, ain't He alright?] [Thank you, Jesus, for my ups and downs] [a second choir member is possessed; the instrumental accompaniment resumes]

As the sermon begins, the pastor's rhythm and tone modulate toward a heightened intensity. Several scholars have noted that music in African and African-American diaspora communities is characterized by an implied beat or rhythmic pulse. The difference between the pastor's speaking cadence in the Biblical lesson and the rhythm which marks the start of the sermon is that during the sermon a sustained pulse is felt that moves beneath a cluster of rhythmic variations. In other words, the implied beat serves a metronomic function. The purpose of this pulse, however, goes beyond the demarcation of time. Rhythm, for African-based cultures, is intimately connected to consciousness and modes of being. Rhythm signals the type of occasion and appropriate behavior as indicated in the expression used by Black people, "He didn't know what time it was," i.e. this person was unaware of the demands of a particular situation or set of affairs, and therefore was unable to give a proper response.

The implied rhythmic pulse not only signals a significant formal shift in the service from teaching to preaching, from lesson to sermon, from community to *communitas*, but creates an entirely distinct atmosphere, moving from concentrated attention to heightened expectation.

Vocal tone and timbre play equally important roles in establishing an environment suffused with kinetic yet contained energy and excitement. The pastor's speech, always expressive with a wide range of vocal contours and color, now assumes a more musical character. His chanted words are almost sung, as his speaking approximates singing yet remains at the threshold of song. As with the implicit pulse, the "pedal-tone" of the pastor's voice is repeated and acts as a tonal center of gravity for the tonal variations to come. The pulse and repeated tone together create a sustained tension. This steady ostinato of pedal-tones is articulated in both verbal and non-verbal form. The verbal utterance is the pastor answering himself after a phrase, just as the deacon shouts his affirmations or exhortations to the members ("Pray Salem" or "Tell the truth"), or as the choir accompanies the soloist, or as a chorus of congregants confirms the truth of the individual's testimony.

[sermon continues]: Jesus said, "Well, what I wish you'd let me do is use this boat, for the multitudes will be here in a moment, and I need to be able to launch it out in the water. I need to be able to launch out into the deep and when I get out into the water, let them be able to hear me expound and expostulate and preach on the word of God. And so, what I want you to do if you don't mind is to let me have your boat."

Simon said, "Well, Lord, this boat is my livelihood. If I lose this boat, I can't feed my family. If I lose this boat, I won't be able to take care of my business. But if you *wan-n-nt* my boat for Kingdom-building and if you want my boat for God's Kingdom, then go on, and take my boat."

And you know what the Bible says, Jesus went on and preached, and *many souls* were saved. And when it was *all over* and the crowd had gone away, I heard, I heard, I *hear-r-rd* [same emphatic tone as "wan-n-nt" in Simon's speech above] Jesus saying:

"*Simon-n-n* [same emphatic tone as above but even louder, more sustained], I'm going to show you now that you can't be 'God-giving' no matter how hard you try."

[Pastor spreads hands, opens handkerchief, turns to the side, immerses handkerchief into waters]:

Here's your boat now,
Get your net,
Drop down on the right side of your boat.

And you know what the Bible says: he dropped the net down and when he got ready to pul-l-l-l up his net, the net broke in half. He couldn't haul in all that he had.

But the point I'm making is that he had to give the boat first. And when you read the Bible, all the way in the Bible, it talks about covenant. It talks about how the different ones made a covenant with God. There was never a covenant made until the giving had been done first. And then when they gave, they asked, and God heard, and answered their prayers.

[Break in tonal continuity: rhythm and inflection in this paragraph resemble those in the earlier teaching lesson] And so as I get ready to leave you today, my brothers and sisters, you must not allow *things* to get in the way between you and God. And you must not allow, you understand, things to be like when the eclipse occurs. The eclipse is when the moon gets between the sun and the earth, and when that happens, that means darkness is upon the face of the earth, and that does not mean, you understand, that the sun has gone out. But the only reason why it's dark on earth is because the moon is between the earth and the sun.

Oh Lord and [whoop = loud intake of air] that's the way it is with us. Mmmmm [whoop], because [whoop] in our lives [whoop] a whole lot of times [Preach, brother] well-l-l-l, uh [whoop], we think, uh [whoop], that God, uh [whoop] has gone away from us. Mmmmm, uh [whoop], and [whoop] we think God [whoop] is nowhere around [whoop], but then [whoop], uh, it's not that God is gone [whoop], my God, [whoop] He's still there, mmmmm [whoop].

But the reason why [whoop] He's not able [whoop] to do for you what He needs to do, um-hmmm [whoop].... [Yeah (sung)] God, you understand [whoop], has too much between Him and you. Oh Lord [moans] [whoop] and [whoop] uh, the things of this world [whoop] that you've allowed yourself to have, *Yes-s-s*, they get down between you and God, Oh Lord.

You need to learn how to trust totally in God, Oh Lord, but too many of us today, we trust anybody and anything before we trust God. Yes we *wil-l-l*. But you're nothing but a steward and whatever it is that you have, God loaned it to you just for a while. Did you hear what I'm saying? My Father will do one of two things [Yeah]: either the Lord will take it away from you, or He'll turn around and take you away from it. Because everything you have is just for a while. Did you hear what I'm saying? Go on wining if you want to, go on dining if you want to, you aren't gonna wine and dine but just for a while. Yes-s-uh, you see, one of these days, you've got to give an accounting of what God gave you. My God, one of these days, the Lord's gonna ask you, "Now what about my house that I gave you, what about my car that you ride, what about my wardrobe?" What will happen then? [choir sings "I Thank You, Lord"]

The sermon has moved from financial to human contingency and mortality. These themes become touchstones of a deeper, more pervasive condition which underlies Black existence, even claiming the consciousness of the middle class, and never out of mind for those with less earning power. The theme of the sermon has returned to human fragility and divine sovereignty, the same themes which shaped the deacon's devotion. Here, however, these themes are expressed through a rhetoric and mode of exhortation which confronts the congregation, while the deacon's prayer service embodies this condition of contingency in ritualized posture and gesture, and finds verbal articulation in prayerful supplication.

The pastor becomes the dramatically enacted voice of God, Jesus, and a host of Bible characters as illustrated by the following scenario. The transition from incidental illustrations to narrative is made by sounding two sung, non-verbal phrases. The first is in the same tone as the concluding phrase of the preceding illustrations; the second introduces the new, modulated tone which will be the new tonal center for the next set of phrases: "I'm gonna leave you when I tell you: 'Ohh.'"

Immediately before he begins the Elijah narrative, the pastor drapes his large white handkerchief over the left shoulder of his dark suit. The connotations of this gesture are rich. The moment signals an intensification of labor, an indication that he is moving even further into the Biblical terrain, closer to the character's presence and thus deeper in the Spirit, which expresses itself through somatic and emotional labors.   Thus Pastor Williams evokes a heightened electric atmosphere of anticipation.

> One day God spoke to the prophet Elijah, "Go down to Zarephath and tell that woman to make me a cake." [My God] The prophet went in and said, "Madam, the Lord told me to tell you, 'Make me a cake.'" I heard her say, "*Noo-o-o-uh.*" Said, "Look here, mister, I don't have anything but a handful of meal and a little cruse of oil. I can't make no cake and give you part of it. I'm gonna make this cake, and me and my son is gonna eat it and die together." [Answers, in tone]: "Yes we will." But I heard him say, "The Lord told me to tell you to make me one first." Yeah, and in faith, don't you see her going to the mill? Got down to the kitchen, poured it out in faith. And God heard, in grace. Did you hear what I'm saying?

The tenses in Pastor Williams' narrative are past and present: "I heard her say...don't you see her going to the mill...She said, 'Look here, mister, I don't have anything but a handful of meal...me and my son is gonna eat it and die together.'" The verbal tenses move within the vocally rhythmic ensemble of the pastor's whooping and the congregation's response. The somatic rhythms of the individual body of the pastor and the collective body of the worshippers create a comprehensive moment for the semantic tenses of the narrative to unfold as present, without the grammatical gravity of the past.   The verbal structure of the pastor's narrative calls and answers, while the non-verbal utterances maintain both the rhythmic pulse and punctuate the narrative.   The tension here is similar to early twentieth-century Afro-American music which depended upon military, four-square marching rhythms, against which musicians placed a contrary, syncopated African rhythm.   The tension-wrought creative freedom born of this rhythmic intercourse eventually became known as jazz. Like the indispensable drummer who holds all time(s) together, the pastor is master of these multiple modes. He becomes the mediatory being whose dramatically enacted witnessing ("I heard her say...") to Elijah, the widow, her son, and God allow the congregation to become immediate participants in the prophetic drama, since one of the crucial purposes of the sermon is to enable everyone to experience God's activity as ongoing and present.

Pastor Williams now picks up the very large pulpit Bible, places it under his arm, and walks across the chancel toward Deacon Sikes on his left. He bends at the words "pouring it out." At the completion of the phrase, he stands, turns 180 degrees, bends again, and says:

While she was pouring it out the topside, heaven was on the backside, shooting it in the bottom. And when she set it down [sets the Bible upright on the pulpit] she had more in the end than she had in the beginning. [He peers down into the top of the Bible which has become transformed into the opening of the vessel containing meal.] That's all I got to tell you–the Lord will provide. I wonder do I have a witness here. The Lor-r-rd will provide, yes He will. It's amazing, how the Lord will provide. He's always, always, always right by my side. Do I have a witness?

The congregation responds at once to the improvisational *tour de force* of the pastor, his craft in action, and are celebrating with him the polished completeness and truth of his dramatic narrative. The theological power and the aesthetic integrity of the performance are inseparable. The pastor's call for a "witness" is both an invitation to the entire congregational body to enter into the celebration of this integral unity of performance and truth, and to bring their own past experiences of the Lord's dependability to bear upon the present demonstration of truth. To witness is not to be spectator or voyeur, but participant. "Do I have a witness?" is a cry to seal the seamless unity between personal past experience and present manifestation with an affirmation of authenticity: Amen!

The pastor's Elijah drama has heightened the level of congregational participation. The choir has become more animated, members are standing, clapping, gesticulating, and shouting their approval.

The congregation is interacting with both the semantic realm of the pastor's utterance and the kinetic body rhythms which are only implied in his cadences and full-throated embellishments. Members sway in time, while their heads move to another more rapid pulse. They express the very simultaneity of presentation that the pastor works masterfully to achieve.

Other responses are not bodily-kinetic but engage the sermon on the level of verbal stylization. For example:

There's no need of trusting in that fine house you have because...
Time you move in, termites starting to eat out your house, My God!
It's no need of trusting that fine 19 and 89 car, because...
This time next year you'll be riding one year behind.

Several members of the choir laugh at the turn of irony in acknowledgement of the truth of the illustration and its undeniable exposure of a believer's vanity. Automobile market research has demonstrated that Black consumers see cars as both a means of transportation and as an extension of their fashion-sense, which is a public presentation of the self.

Others, however, have been engaging the sermon at both its musical and affective tonal level. Expressing non-verbally the same rise and fall of minor modes, the pastor has sustained the emotional tenor of his sermon. "There's no need in trusting in that fine house you have... Well yeah!" The tendency is to understand these expressions as either mirrors of the pastor's mood and feeling, or to see them as responses. I have considered both and tend toward understanding them as expressions of a collective mood, rather than the aggregation of discrete responses. In other words, the articulation of one expressive utterance does not mean that the person has eliminated or excluded the others. A member may be caught up in the mournful dimensions of the sermon, yet be aware of the humorous diversion present in another member's laughter. The purpose of this moment in the service is the fullness of simultaneous possibilities of mood, response, expression and utterance; or the creative exploration of liminality which feeds the creation and life of communities. Black expression is a form of commitment and focus. The voices which answer the pastor in a high, musical wail are selectively responding to the mournful dimension of his presentation. These voices, however, are not re-presenting the pastor's emotions. The sounds express personal responses to the sermon while also serving as embodiments of the story's tragic dimension. The members' actions, therefore, have their origins in both evocations and expression. Belonging to both, they are the exclusive dominion of neither.

Following the series of illustrations, Pastor Williams concludes with a reiteration of themes:

> You've got to trust in God... [Yes, ya' have]
> You've got to trust in-n-n God [dropping tone]
> You've got to trust in God—I don't believe you hear me...

At this point one of the deacons stands and facing the pulpit, opens his arms, lifting them in a wide vertical arch, and claps his hands together three times, punctuating one of the many implied rhythms which now saturate the entire sanctuary.

> The Lord will provide, yes He will. It's amazing how the Lord will provide. He [screaming] is al-l-l-lways, al-l-l-lways, al-l-l-lways [the organ, bass and saxophone enter for the first time] right by my side. Do I have a witness? [The instrumentalists are now speaking back and improvising within the suggested tonal clusters of the pastor's chanted notes.]

When the pastor says "my side," he is speaking both for himself and the congregation. The personal pronouns have become both individual and collective in the shared enactment of the religious drama.

The congregation's affirmation and experiences of God's presence and life-sustaining reliability stand in diametric contrast, almost theologically antagonistic, to the understanding of a deity who sits exalted in heaven, whose worshippers gathered in mournful submission at the foot of His altar, kneeling before a rude chair. Western intellection addressed this problem through the creation of Trinitarian theology, which was the result of wrestling with a Greek philosophical conception of Jesus. Afro-Christianity has been influenced by this aspect of Western Christianity. Traditional Black Christianity owes its vitality not to the philosophically based formulations of the great Christian doctrines but to the existential encounter with God in all His peculiar modes of being which resist logical resolution.

On the level of theologically discursive understanding, the mode of divine being encountered in the deacon's devotion is in contradiction to the enacted, proclaimed and affirmed immanent reliability of God's presence and action experienced at this point of the worship. Western liturgical responses gather multiple dimensions of meaning into symbols and hold these realms in tension-wrought and paradoxical unity. The Afro-Christian mode of understanding embraces polyvalent dimensions of existence and meaning through enacted and articulated simultaneity. Symbols have a contemplative dimension wherein one reflects upon or encounters them repeatedly, as for example, the sacramental body of Christ broken, again and again, at each Eucharist. But this ritualized presentation of symbol strives toward noetic comprehension and inner experience. One may be exhorted to "act out the Eucharist" in daily life. "This mass has ended, go and serve the Lord." But one does not act out the Eucharist during its celebration. One internalizes it, literally and noetically. In contrast, Afro-American worship invites, indeed depends upon embodied enactment rather than upon symbolic representation.

Pastor Williams now points to the congregation and says, "I don't know what I would do without the Lord. I wonder do I have a witness here?" He then unbuttons his coat and says, "He's been mighty good to me." He places his thumb in his waistband and says, "I could have been dead [modulating], sleeping in my grave, Oh-h-h-h-, the Lo-r-r-rd made death behave." He is simultaneously celebrating the pastoral proximity to God necessary for any Black preacher to fulfill his role, and confirming the congregation's experience of divine-human dependency. At this point Pastor Williams has reached the spiritual posture and attitude of the deacons before the God who lifts people up and lays them down, who gives life and takes it away. His open coat and proclamation of gratitude place him in a disposition akin to that of the deacons, without having to remove his jacket or assume their posture of kneeling. In other words, he is re-situating the relationship of radical contingency powerfully portrayed in the deacon's devotion, now placed within the environment of praise and gratitude, which affirms and portrays the reliability and constancy of God's companionship.

The pastor is exposing both mournful gratitude and anguished ecstasy at the mercy and power of God, for which His present moment of existence is undeniable evidence.   "A-a-a-h-h-h, The Lord, ummmmm" Mourning, fear, supplication, anguish–the pastor is gathering the deep-seated feelings born of Black believers' affliction, and laboring to transform their ecstasy, celebration and praise. Bending his knees and stooping while looking up at the balcony, the pastor cries out:

> "A-a-a-ah-h-h...I know! I feel alright, Deacon Napper. Soul on fire, talking about money, and how people ought to provide. Didn't think I'd feel like this."

Pastor Williams is unmasking, becoming confessional, hence performing the verbal parallel to the previous gesture of divesting by speaking intimately to the trusted and reliable chair of the Deacon Board.

> Thank you Jesus, for my ups and downs,
> for my mountains and my valleys.
> But my God is amazing. He's been so good to me.
> I look back [whoop]
> Not no whole lot of years [whoop]
> But just go thirty days back. [saxophone answers]
> I wanted the land over yonder. [whoop]
> I said, "Well now, Lord [whoop]
> if you give me that land [whoop]
> I promise you [whoop]
> I'll give it back to you." [saxophone answers]
> And here I am, thirty days later
> Got the land [whoop] [extends left hand, then pulls back]
> Got money [whoop] [repeats gesture with right hand]
> Look at me [whoop] [repeats gesture with left hand]
> I'm doing alright! [Rev. Sypho pats the pastor on his shoulder several times]

This segment of the service is a dramatic aside, couched in the form of a personal confession, since the primary address is to Deacon

Napper. The congregation seems to be only the indirect audience. Deacon Napper is perhaps one of the most trustworthy members of the congregation. Members often go to him with privileged information, for counsel and prayer. He is also an elder to Pastor Williams, who relies upon his wisdom and confidence as well.

In the style of masterful Black American improvisatory artists in several creative venues, Pastor Williams has taken his original theme into a new setting. He is connecting his personal testimony with the theme of the Wednesday night prayer service. The technique is similar to that of jazz musicians who play identical phrases in a variety of harmonic environments (hear Miles Davis on ESP). But Pastor Williams' presentation is guided by the theology of exaltation, which shapes human weakness into a cause for celebration. Immediately following his phrase "I'm doing alright!" comes "Ain't He alright?" The question is as much declarative as interrogatory, an invitation to praise in the face of power.

> Yes sir!
> Ahhhhh!!! Ahhhhh!!!
> The Lord is...
> Ahhhhhh!!!
> The Lord is...
> Ahhhhhh, the Lord is!!!!
> Ahhhhh!!! [bending toward the floor]
> He will... [pause]

The musicians are no longer answering but are improvising their own obbligatos like an instrumental sermon. The pianist is repeating ascending chords. Nearly the entire choir is standing and waving their arms, indicating the presence of the Spirit. The congregation, long since animated in their seats, is beginning to rise. The pastor returns the microphone to its stand on the pulpit, but before it is settled in place he removes it again and continues:

> Yes sir! [the instrumentalists return to answering his phrases]
> Yes Sir!
> Ahhhh!!!
> Ahhhh...w-w-w-won't He
> won't He make a way?
> W-w-w-won't He
> open doors for you?
> W-w-w-won't He give you power
> wrapped in His hand?
> Ahhhh!!!
> I know He will.

The encounter with the numinous is made by the individual, but the journey is undertaken by the community. The congregation enters into the pastor's experience, confirming the truth of his testimony out of their own experiential knowledge. The pastor directly addresses the congregation, declaring the universal applicability of his personal encounter. At the same time, he is inviting them to affirm their own sense of divine reliability as he expresses the identical character of their empirical knowledge. "We are following and sharing the same God."

Unity is achieved by sharing the core of one's experience of God, an invitation to entry into each other's personal religious drama, through the reciprocity of affirmation and invitation. Boundaries have been collectively dissolved.

The pastor, in a protracted gesture, wipes his mouth with the handkerchief draped over his shoulder. All, including the pastor, are sustained in the effulgent ambiance of what they have created together. The musicians are playing open-ended chords and phrases which do not resolve. In other words, they are perpetuating the mood and extending the truth of the moment. For even though a significant moment in the sermon has been completed, it is not yet concluded. Members are swaying, dancing to rhythms which are unheard but find articulation only in their bodies. Everyone has arrived at the fullness of engaged anticipation. We are at a threshold, suspended between and sustained by the morning's liturgical labors and the open expectancy of the afternoon's conclusion.

> I know He will [pastor moves slowly away from the pulpit toward Deacon Napper]
> He's alright [cymbal crash; pastor returns the emphasis]
> Thank you, Holy Spirit [pastor puts his hand in his pocket and dips]
> He's al-l-lright [instrumental obbligato in response]
> Would y'all help me say that one more time?
> He's al-l-l-lright [organ enters with sustained chord]

This is an important alternative in the musical textures, for as capable of sustaining notes or chords as the bass, piano and saxophone may be, their effect has to be repeated, or in the example of the saxophone, is confined to single-line phrases. The organ enters with sustained fullness which swells and fills the sanctuary. The sound is visceral and envelops everyone, gathering everyone into and providing shape for the new environment which has been collectively created. The organ is the acoustic bridge into the next phrase of worship: ecstatic *communitas*.

Several members scattered throughout the congregation stand, move, applaud, give joyful utterance. As the pastor repeats, "He's al-l-l-l-right," this time the members join in, creating a large chordal harmony, following the pastor through the vocal ascent of the phrase, except that he stops singing before the resolution, stands, and allows the congregation to finish the phrase. People are joyfully entering the transitional stage of the service, as the pastor creates space for them to claim the moment as fully their own, a shared creation. Shrieks of joy rise up. Smiles multiply. Some members are wiping tears with white linen, others are rocking back and forth in fluent rhythms of excitement. The pastor turns to Deacon Napper's side of the chancel.

Somebody didn't say it [points]
Somebody way over yonder didn't say it [turns to the opposite side and points]
Somebody up there didn't say it [points to the balcony]
If you know the Lord has made a way for you, just one more time, help me say it...
He's al-l-l-llright!
[An elderly woman stands, turns, circles in place, then runs up the length of the center aisle, then back down, only to repeat her path in ceaseless motion.]
He's al-l-l-llright! [leaps an octave, then bends down, almost touching the ground, vocally exhausted, voice breaking]
Ain't He alright!? Ain't He got power!? [drum and cymbal crash]
Ooooooooohhhhh! [screaming, then locates musical pitch and begins to sing]
He's al-l-l-lright
He's a-l-l-l [stops again and allows the congregation to complete the phrase]

The pastor's posture of praise is achieved through the expenditure of his own power, the declaration of his status, through gestures and confession and the laudatory, emphatic "He's alright," which is not a modest tribute in the Black vernacular. "Alright" embraces a totality and wholeness which leaves nothing to be desired, as in: "The girl's alright with me, you know the girl's alright" (Temptations) or "Baby, everything's alright, up tight, clean out of sight" (Stevie Wonder).

The dimension of God articulated in the physical attitudes of supplication and dread–God's ineluctable and ambiguous power–has now been shaped into the service of the community: sustaining resources for ministry and survival. God is, therefore, worthy of joyful praise, in contrast to the mournful praise of the deacons. From supplication to celebration.

The pastor now launches the vehicle which will take us from expectancy to ecstasy. Without any previous announcement he chooses an appropriate song from the formidable catalogue of his memory: "We....[long pause; congregation sings antiphonal 'we'] are our Heaven-n-ly Father's children." The congregation recognizes the hymn. Its loping beat leaves ample space for interaction and is a broad invitation for participation. The meter is 6/8. The entire congregation begins to sing, the first collective hymn since the service opened. But unlike the significance of the congregation's service, however, the members have transposed interior and interpersonal boundaries, reaching the inner depths where feelings reside available to the broader membership through their affective, noetic and somatic engagement and articulation. This hymn, unlike the others, will not create community but will express the condition of *communitas* and allow for the experience of ecstasy which is but one, albeit radical, expression of *communitas*.

[Pastor]: And we all know
that He loves us, one and all.
Yet there are times
We find our answer.

All of the deacons are standing, with Deacon Napper extending his arm and free hand in an arc which sweeps the sanctuary. Women and men are weeping, while adjacently seated members offer each other consolation, an embrace, rhythmically curving the back, fanning others who have been overcome. Others are smiling, shouting praise, rejoicing through their tears. The variegated palette of the human condition emerges in an atmosphere conducive to the expression of contradictory experience and equally contradictory responses. The leveling of status, office, rank and posture is inseparable from the emergence of seemingly disparate affective realms. The sanctuary, unlike the work place, the home, or the market, has been transformed into a situation which does not require repression or splitting of feelings.

Men and women are exchanging roles. Women, who are socially expected and culturally licensed to weep under stress and grief, and in general allowed a more demonstrative expressive and affective life, become empathic comforters to men who have collapsed into sobbing heaps. For men, the public display of intimate feelings, pain, and vulnerability accompanied by tears or weeping is generally censored. For a Black man, the public display of feelings is not only censored, but calls into question his fundamental identity as a male, while his state of vulnerability places him at risk.

Oh-h-h-h-h
If you are willing
the Lord will teach us
The Heavenly Father will
always answer prayer
He knows–I'm so glad He knows–
He knows
Just [congregation answers: just]
How much [congregation answers: how much]
I can bear. [That's what I like about Him, children]

The hymn has called forth the experience of desperation, of suffering the incessant reminders of human finitude, into a context that was created by the unanimous praise and celebration of God's trustworthiness and reliability.

The deity of incalculable power, capable of creating and destroying the cosmos, who was encountered and implored in the deacon's devotion, praised broadly in the congregational service, and whose Son was specifically described and created in the pastor's service, is revealed as having discernable contours to the use of His inestimable power which we know as suffering. Suffering is not considered the work of Satan, rather God is being indirectly acknowledged as the source of and deliverer from affliction. During worship, divine character assumes the deep strata and powerful suppleness of African rhythms, the polyangularity of African sacred sculpture, the richness of harmonic nuance in jazz.

You ought to think [points to his head]
of the times
you've asked the question
down in your heart,
"Lord, what shall I do?"
I can't go to my friends
[spoken: don't want to worry nobody]
And you can't go to your loved ones
They have their troubles too
[spoken: but guess what]
Ther-r-r-re is a God [rising toward a scream, pointing to heaven, raises arms to shoulder level]
Who rules earth and heaven and
In Him there is relief of every pain and care
He kno-w-w-w-w-s
Oh-h-h-h-h
I'm so glad He knows [congregation answers: sing it, sing, sing]
Just [congregation answers: just]
How much

I can bear.

A choir member who has been rocking back and forth, holding her head with her hand, suddenly stands, moves down the row of seats and leaves. An attentive fellow choir member seizes the microphone pinned to the distraught member's robe, quickly unclasps it, thus sparing her sister certain entanglement. Members are raising their hands, verifying the sudden visitation of the Holy Spirit.

[Spoken]: "Do you know that I'm gonna leave you when I tell you... the load, the load, the load-d-d get heavy."

The pastor walks toward his musicians, back erect, eyes toward heaven, inclining further with each word. On the first articulation of "the load," he unfurls his handkerchief which has been wrapped around the microphone in his right hand. On the second articulation, he drops it over his left shoulder, stooping almost to the floor under the weight of a suggested cross. At the end of the word, he stands again, punctuating the phrase and ending the service. He then turns, faces the congregation, points, and says:

But you remember, you ain't never
left alone to bear it all
[spoken rapidly: just get down on your knees, children, and just tell
Him] [almost level to ground]
Just ask for strength, and keep on toiling [spoken: keep on] though
the teardrops are going to fall
Ah-h-h
You-o-o-u have the joy
of His assurance
the Heavenly Father
will always answer prayer.
He knows [rhythm changes here to a more joyful rock]
Ohh-h-h-h
I'm so-o-o glad He knows
He knows just how much
He knows just how much
He knows just how much
He knows jus-s-st how much
He knows jus-s-st how much
[spoken]: I couldn't stand no more...
Just how much
He knows just-s-st how much
We can bear-r-r

Members have their eyes closed, shaping the rhythms with their bodies, stroking the air, swaying back and forth hypnotically. Members are still ministering to one another, to the mournful, enraptured, overwhelmed. Many exclaim, "Thank You Jesus, Thank You Jesus." At the pastor's last phrase, "We can bear-r-r," he severely retards the rhythm and the congregation breaks into applause. The organ hits a sustained chord, the saxophone rises, the cymbals are sounding. Most of the members are standing. In the midst of this sustain, the pastor beckons:

> The door of the Lord's house is open for you to come [deacons step forward and face the congregation]
> Will you come to church?
> Will you join the church and receive my Jesus as your personal Savior, will you come?
> [as the organ continues its sustain, the pastor rolls his hands in the air and begins another song]
> Ohh-h-h-h, everything [the choir, now standing, responds: everything]
> Is gonna be alright
> [spoken]: Let's open them [the doors] this way... everybody on your feet, the doors of the church is open, and please, nobody walk out
> Ohh-h-h-h [the congregation stands]
> After the storm cloud passes over
> Everyone is gonna be alright
> Everything
> Ohh-h-h-h everything

Everyone is singing and clapping in rhythm to the redefined unity. The congregation has moved into and through the deepest center of its common affliction. The feelings and conditions which arise out of desperate circumstances, the helplessness, the overwhelming demands of mediating the posture and material confirmation of disparity, the day-to-day stresses of confronting expressions of racism which remind one of the devalued worth of Black life in the eyes of most Americans, the day-to-day risk of violence which for Black people is more likely to emerge in the most intimate and familiar spaces of the home and neighborhood, and whose agents are more likely to be acquaintances, friends or relatives, have been exorcised not by the pastor alone, but through the creative collective interactions and contributions, both spontaneous and rehearsed, of the congregation. The consummate creation in the service, the mutual and responsive work of God and worshippers is, in the end, not symbols but community and cosmos.

Traditional patterns and attitudes which characterize the worship of Afro-Christians entail the labor of creatively locating, intelligently shaping, and bodily manifesting the internalized forces which injure, alienate, and debilitate–forces which, if left unarticulated, and, more importantly, unshared, will either prohibit or destroy the possibility of healing community. The genius of traditional worship among Black Christians can be identified in their approach to these potentially destructive elements, which are endemic and were often beyond the control of most Black Americans. Their gift and precious life-giving resource is to embrace the very core of injury and transform its destructive pathology into the divine energy of ecstatic communion through the profoundly sophisticated forms of creative suffering.   In giving this suffering aesthetic dramatic and interpretive shape, worshippers enable it and themselves to participate in a different, more expansive dimension of self, suffering, and God. The irony involved in this metamorphosis is that they must have a community in order to achieve *communitas*. And to have a community, one must possess some basic perceptual and intuitive sense of one's relatedness to others, a fundamental relational ontology. We have achieved ecstatic *communitas*, through which cosmos is born.

> [Pastor]: Everything is gonna be alright, alright, alright
> [congregation claps in rhythm and responds: alright]
> Oh-h-h-h, after
> [after]
> storm
> [storm cloud]
> passes over
> [over]
> everything
> [everything's gonna]
> be-e-e
> [be alright]
> You put your trust in Him [pointing to heaven], in Him, oh Lordy,
> even, even when the light grows dim, oh-h-h-h after
> [after]
> storm
> [storm cloud passes]
> over
> [o-o-o-ver]
> ev-er-y-thing
> [everything's gonna be alright]
> Alright, alright, I said everything
> [everything]
> gonna be
> [gonna be alright]

Pastor Williams motions are dancelike. His steps take him across the chancel, gliding gracefully. The economy of his motions and the strength of their suggestion carry far greater weight than were he to become overly animated. The power of his movement resides in its understated choreography.

A-a-a-after storm
  [after storm cloud pass]
over
  [o-o-o-over]
everything
  [everything's gonna be alright]
Oh-h-h-h, everything
  [everything]
gonna
  [gonna be alright]
alright, alright, I said everything
  [everything]
gonna be
  [gonna be alright]
Oh-h-h-h-h after
  [after storm cloud passes]
after trouble
  [after storm cloud passes]
after trial
  [after storm cloud passes]
after tribulation
  [after storm cloud passes]
after heartaches [dances back across the chancel]
  [after storm cloud passes]
after heartbreak
  [after storm cloud passes]
after after sickness sickness [doubling the rhythm]
  [after storm cloud passes]
after trouble, trouble, trouble, trouble, trouble
  [after storm cloud passes]
after storms, after storms
  [after storm cloud passes]
after cloudy days
  [after storm cloud passes]
over
  [over]
everything
  [everything's gonna be alright]

The series of repeated phrases beginning with "after..." establishes a suspended moment, similar to the previous occurrences in the worship. This one occurs, however, at a point wherein the condition of *communitas* is at its apogee. These patterns establish the rhythm and emotional setting for possession, which can occur at any point in the service with or without the pastor's presence. Yet possession is but the expression within the relational terrain of *communitas*. These rhythms heighten tension by building and prolonging rhythmic irresolution. The Spirit overtakes a female member of the choir in the second row. Her body lurches forward, bending at the waist, both arms extended over her head, then she catapults backwards to an upright position. She rapidly repeats this motion before falling into her seat. She is lurching backwards over her seat, her motion too sudden and violent to permit her fellow choir members to approach with comforting assistance. They stand out of the reach of her volcanic flailing until she collapses onto the floor. Two members, one male and one female, bend to lift her motionless body.

Pastor Williams smiles, facing forward, unaware of the drama of the Spirit behind his back, and says, "Ain't nobody mad but the Devil!" His statement is richly poetic for he is signaling both the manifestation of the Spirit in all its pervasiveness, encompassing fullness, who has touched most of the members and whose power cannot be resisted. The consequence of its omnipresence is a concomitant diminution of the Devil's influence, power and presence. Concomitant for the primary interest of the service is not the ritualized address and assault upon the demonic, yet the Spirit's presence has, nevertheless, performed a collective and indirect exorcism of the demonic.

Pastor Williams' comment, however, also contains a veiled exhortation and reprimand, for the comment is addressed to a small, motionless pocket, perhaps the only remaining one in the vibrantly swaying sanctuary. He is personifying the demonic presence by making indirect reference to the recalcitrant members who statically resist the ocean of motion around them. He has brilliantly enrolled the two agents of divisiveness whose actions are contrary to the literal moment of Spirit of the entire worship service, into the service of unity and wholeness.

Pastor Williams' next statement claims ownership for the direct intent of the previous one and reveals his intention: "If you are not too mean, you ought to put your hands together." He glides across the chancel; musicians are improvising melodically and rhythmically, taking advantage of the open space and building the intensity. Members are weeping, rejoicing, clapping in rhythm.

"Shake hands, shake hands, and tell 'em, 'Don't worry, everything is gonna be alright!"

Members clap hands and swing their arms back and forth joyously. Pastor Williams turns slightly, and travels across the chancel to the opposite side.

"Go on the other side now, and tell' em, 'Don't worry, everything will be alright.'"

He executes a side-shuffle, a dance of celebration and confident rejoicing in the felt presence and reliability of the Lord's comfort. He arrives at the pulpit, places the microphone in its stand. Another member becomes the site of the Spirit's powerful entry. The pastor sings, "Everything's gonna be al-right, everything's gonna..." He is joined by the inspirational singers in bringing this phase of the service to an end. Applause. The organ holds a full chord, saxophone still intoning, cymbals sustaining, piano holding, bass running. Members continue to shriek, "Lord, ooo-o-o-oh." The drummer returns to the pulse, the saxophone creates a new melody, supported by bass, organ and piano. The congregation won't let the rhythm's movement end, the music resolve, or the Spirit rest. The pastor acknowledges the gift: "Thank You Jesus!" [Halleluyah] "Thank You *Jesus*!" Although the members have returned to the pews, another member is caught up in the spirit.

For my ups and downs! For my mountains and my valleys!

The pastor's expression of gratitude suggests that the goal of worship has been achieved, the dismantling of boundary between affliction and comfort, gratitude and grievance, injury and healing, oppression and celebration. All distillations have achieved an equanimity, inner and outer, status and stigma, individual and community have exchanged positions and as a result have lost their discrete identity. The devastating injury and the worldly defense of power, rank and alienation have been eroded by the transformative power of the sacred. But this experience of the sacred is not the Holy Other of Rudolf Otto[1] and Western understanding, but of African dimensions. Zeuss[2] speaks of African religions as religions of structure, which is the result of transferring otherness into the structure of everyday life.

But African-Americans, Black American Africans of the North American Diaspora, historically have not controlled the structures of their lives or been able to integrate their experience across the strains of economic, political and family life in the manner of the grand African religions. Cult and pantheon have their deities and accompanying priests to stitch the world and personal experience together.

The North American Black Christian has experienced discontinuity and rupture in the most profoundly intimate and primary realms of his life. The interpersonal intensities of family, marriage, procreation and community have been beyond his collective or individual control. This historical condition has profoundly shaped and altered the understanding and appropriation of the displaced African's religious heritage. The realm of his control was not structure but ritual; the telos of his worship was not the establishment of distinct cults in a larger religious system made up of various practices including divination, possession, healing, et al. Rather the telos of his worship and practice became confined to the creation of cultic community. But from within this cauldron of suffering he created the crucible of *communitas*, which in turn redefined both his African and Christian inheritance, each with distinctive definitions and experiences of the sacred. The Black American created a new understanding of Spirit, one which is lost where the understanding of worship is in terms of a narrow and exclusive focus upon possession. Between the Protestant encounter with the Holy Other, the Catholic sacramental encounters with the symbolic and real presence, and the African religion of structure, is the Black American creation of relational sacrality. The experience of the Spirit is better understood as both personal and collective, as that force, or more accurately, assemblage of simultaneously interactive forces and conditions, which result in the multiple collapse of boundaries. The Spirit may be experienced privately, but the goal of worship is to create the conditions, which enable the presence to be known (in the Biblical Hebraic sense of knowing) as a communal reality, which re-determines all of the experiences and categories of perception.

The Holy, in this sense, addresses all of the senses at once, and invites, often demands irresistibly a visceral, collectively enacted response. An illustration of this activity can be observed in Salem's response to a person in the throes of possession. One of the members of the Usher Board and the choir member described earlier became possessed. The Usher Board member left her seat, and in her paroxysms began to dance, her arms flailing but her steps inventive, orderly, rhythmic. The choir member was accompanied to the front of the church from the choir loft. Usher and lay members gathered about each woman still in the height of their possession. Holding up their arms, their bodies moved with the trashing, indecipherable yet recognizable gestures of the Spirit's animation. The embodied otherness of the Holy Spirit's manifestation in the two women became the shared, conjoined enactments of cellular communities of comfort and nurture gathered about each of them. The possessed members' movements began to assume a more conventional form. The members of the comforting cell around each began to dance with them, interacting and interpreting their movements. Finally both cells became engaged in a unique but shared dance, the creation of the possessed individual and the comforting community. The order of this experience follows the description of Zeuss who contends that African responses to the Holy move from otherness to structure, but the movement here is from otherness to community. The cellular activities of the comforting ministers contributes to the more pervasive sense of *communitas*. But the individual's experience of the Holy Other was but one particular manifestation of the experience of the Spirit's presence, a presence invited and enabled by the Spirit's creation of transformed relationships within the context of social intimacy.

The pastor brings the moment to an end by chanting:

Everybody who love the Lord say
Yes
 [Yes]
Everybody should say
Yes
 [Yes]
Yes Lord
Everybody say Amen
[Amen]
Everybody say Amen
[Amen]
Everybody say Amen
[Amen]
Everybody say Amen
[Amen]
Everybody say Amen
[Amen]
Everybody say Amen
[Amen]
Give God a hand, will ya?
[applause, concluding obbligatos]

I want to thank you for honoring our requests, only one or two walked out. Thank you so much. What a church, what a people. ["It's gonna be alright!" someone screams in a voice full of wretched insistence.]

The pastor prepares the congregation to share the offering. The final ceremony is the welcoming of new members, the benediction, and the recess. Pastor Williams leaves with a few deacons through a special door. Then the choir and musicians conclude the service. Members of the congregation either retire to the fellowship room or go to their cars.

Chapter 4

Phenomenological Interpretation

Towards a Phenomenological Theology of Traditional Afro-Christian Worship

What, then, are we to make of this corpus of material? One could impose the categories of systematic theology, i.e. pneumatology, soteriology, Christology, and engage the material from the perspective of classical theological discourse. Another version of this exercise would detect recent liberation motifs in the prayers, music, sermon and rituals of the service. The worship would find historical continuity with the religious experience of the slaves who proleptically acted out their longing for freedom under conditions of suffering servitude. Either of these strategies, or any other theological examination, I contend, prematurely directs the material into alignment with theological positions, which may or may not belong to the moments recorded at Salem Baptist Church.

Phenomenology has a crucial role to play in theological investigations. Tillich reminds us that "theology must apply the phenomenological approach to all its basic concepts."[1] I agree wholeheartedly, would include a phenomenological investigation of "theology" itself, and theology as a "concept" with its embedded noetic tilt, following Husserl's direction of moving from the abstract to the acts in an effort to uncover layers of sedimented meaning.

Traditional Afro-Christianity is at heart experientially rooted. This is not to relegate or ignore the pluralities within the various Christian traditions within North America. Rather, the effort is to distinguish the Afro-Christian tradition which depends upon aural acquisition and oral transmission of the Bible from communities which emphasize typographic-textualized interpretations or which understand the Bible as a sacramental object within the context of a rite. Among Afro-

Christians, encounters between the deity and the believer are the determining moment in their faith and relationship with God. While African-Christian communities developed highly poetic understandings of God, which their members can express in thoughtful, eloquent articulation, their primary referent is neither doctrine, catechism nor systematic theology, but experience and the wisdom derived from proverbs, adages, testimony, hymnody, aphorism and memorized scripture. For this study I have limited my investigation to the prayer and worship service. I have treated the prayer service as a form of worship, but with the distinguishing elements of personal testimony which allow the service to include and address far more of the member's private needs and experiences.

The place to begin to construct a theological understanding of traditional Afro-Christian worship is not theology in our contemporary sense, but the point of entry is a recovery, or better, uncovering of the primary experiences of prayer and worship. Husserl's dictum "to the things" provides a reliable starting point. Spiegelberg understands this to be the common denominator among the varied assemblage of phenomenologists. Spiegelberg understands *Zu dem Sachem* as:

> a fresh approach to the concretely experienced phenomena, as free as possible from conceptual presuppositions, and an attempt to describe them as faithfully as possible...

> Its original meaning was that phenomenology aims...at a direct investigation of the phenomena. Its peculiar thrust was to get away from the primacy of theories, concepts, and symbols, to immediate contact with the intuited data of experience.[2]

Experience is the *Sachem* or "things" which receive the intensive and intuitive scrutiny of phenomenologists. "Thing" is used in a highly qualified sense, for unlike the tradition of British and Anglo-American philosophy and science, phenomenology does not divorce the object of observation from the observer, but strives toward interpretation of the encounter. For the phenomenologists, persons are never simply observers but participants in a unified experience of the phenomenal world.

Don Ihde, acknowledging the experiential center of phenomenological inquiry, identifies two related but distinct orders of phenomenology: "first phenomenology" and "second phenomenology."[3]

> First phenomenology often yields an early appreciation of the richness and complexity of experience.[4]

The aim of the first form of phenomenology is to make as precise as possible the shape of the experience being investigated.[5]

Husserl is the towering figure identified by Ihde with this form.

For Husserl the center of attention and of all experience is intentionality, that essence of experience to be directed towards, to be "aimed" at. And in first phenomenology, the concern is to take note of, to describe and analyze the ways that directedness takes place in both language and perceptual and imaginative experience.[6]

Experience is always experience of something, just as consciousness is consciousness of something. First phenomenology makes the moment, the event, the evanescent emergence wherein human experience is to be found its primary data. Second phenomenology is associated by Ihde with the work of Heidegger.

Second phenomenology begins where first phenomenology leaves off. It takes for granted the attainments of phenomenological method in its most radical sense and directs its questions to both an extension and a deepening of the formal ontologies of Husserl toward a fundamental ontology of Being. Its aim is that of a hermeneutic and existential philosophy.[7]

Heidegger understood that inquiry into human experience revealed more than "pure" experience. Experience and perception are shaped by history, culture, language.

For while the first word of phenomenology is addressed to the nearness of experience as a philosophy of presence, second phenomenology is a rebound which opens the way to a re-evaluation and re-examination of the very language in which our experience is encased and by which it is expressed. The phenomenology of essence, structure, and presence in Husserl leads to the phenomenology of existence, history, and the hermeneutical in Heidegger.[8]

First and second phenomenology are two stages in the phenomenological task: description and interpretation. Another way of presenting the relationship between the two phenomenologies is to think of the first as the *epoche* of the second. While the task never achieves perfection, nevertheless one attempts to reveal experience accurately in temporary suspension of their cultural and historical continuity.

First phenomenology often yields an early appreciation of the richness and complexity of experience. But second phenomenology in pursuing that richness discerns in the sedimentation of our traditions of thought an essential embodiment in history and time of experience itself.[9]

For this study, however, history and time are embedded within experience. Ihde tends to treat "time" and "history" in the manner of the great European philosophers, i.e. as independent subjects. For my study, time and history are embedded within the human subject and become mediated by worship and prayer.

In light of Ihde's distinctions, I have attempted to provide a first phenomenology of traditional Afro-Christian worship. My intention is to construct a phenomenology of this religious experience, which would in time permit an examination of the language, methods, and means through which this experience emerges into the present. Second phenomenology focuses upon the realm of experience which is unthought of by the participants, and therefore becomes a self-conscious reflection upon the relationship between language and experience.

The point of linkage between a first and second phenomenology of traditional Afro-Christian worship is the question of divine presence. Phenomenology emphasizes that experience is experience of something. If first phenomenology is a "philosophy of experience,"[10] then it is also a "philosophy of presence."

Our first question asked from this perspective becomes: what in the context of traditional Afro-Christian worship is presence? Here we arrive at our first sedimentary layer of culture and metaphysics. For I am asking this question of presence of an experience which has already undergone radical alteration. We have taken an event, in this case the act of worship and prayer, with its multiple simultaneous interactions, utterances and enactments of the gathered assembly, and transcribed those events into a text. The latter term in contemporary, i.e. post-modern, usage, is highly ambiguous. "Text" no longer refers to this monograph, the printed page before the reader, the empirical object to be examined. "Text" can be any system of signs subject to interpretation: cinema, laws, rituals, fashion, customs, etc. Text no longer refers to signified objective reality: reality is discourse. The shift is from a referential system of meaning (sign-signified), with the accompanying logocentric metaphysics which made the text a dependable mediator of meaning, to a differential theory of language. Language becomes a system of opposing signs wherein meaning is never found in reference to a realm outside the text, for the logocentric metaphysic upon which the West historically relied as the ultimate reference and source of meaning has been deconstructed and seen only as that which was posited.

> The deconstruction of "sign" leaves us not with a presence but with the trace of a time; and by the same token, the deconstruction of any signifying system—a consciousness, a society, an epoch, or whatever—leaves us with a text, a differential network, a fabric of traces referring and leading to something other than itself, to other differential traces.[11]

Our contemporary understanding of text denies the existence of presence in the text. Previous systems used the text to refer to presence in any number of realms: the mind, realm of eternal forms (ideas), matter. What both systems of meaning—referential and differential—hold in common, however, is the conviction that reality ultimately resides outside of experience.

Phenomenology enters this dispute from a different vantage point and with a different focus. Phenomenology attempts to make understandable "acts whose meaning presents itself only in the actual performance."[12] This insight is crucial both to the general understanding of phenomenology and to the immediate task of providing a hermeneutical phenomenology of prayer and worship. Phenomenology understands language not as a system of signs (anti-metaphysic) or as a system of fixed references (metaphysic), but as an event, an act, an experience. In the context of worship, this distinction cannot be over-emphasized for language is always embodied and enacted. Even when the sacred book is present, the Bible is not treated as a sacramental object but as a corpus which must be uttered, enacted, brought to life in a particular style of communally sanctioned and recognized elocutionary acts. The question and status of presence, which concerns the deconstructionists, logocentric metaphysicians, and phenomenologists, is best understood as a transient experience which is enacted and received.

Our investigation, therefore, attends to the question of presence in language in relationship to three foci: as used in the ritual context of prayer and worship; community; and the sacred.

Language: Sense and Sensorium

It doesn't take much to create drama in the Black community, just say
the word "tree," and bam! you've got a tree growing on stage.
–Ntozake Shange, PBS interview, 1979

It is obvious that most civilized people are crude and numb in their
perceptions, compared with the hyperaesthesia of oral and auditory
cultures. –Marshall McLuhan, *The Gutenberg Galaxy.*

We must first recognize that the word as a printed object and the
word as utterance belong to different orders of reality and two different
communities. Communities which still hold the spoken word in high
regard experience words as an event, an experience, as presence distinct
from those who understand the word as sign, printed or uttered. The
distinction cannot rest exclusively between literate and oral. While
Black American Christians come from religious traditions which trace
their African and New World origins in communities of primary
orality, contemporary Black believers inhabit a world of heterogeneous
orality. The term identifies not only populations which have members
who are literate, and others who depend primarily upon spoken
communication, but members who are not only literate who whose
sensibilities and fundamental orientation remain closer to the values
and perspectives of primary orality. Important to note is that Ntozake
Shange (in the epigraph quoted above) was addressing a gathering of
Black people who had read and attended the performance of her play
*For Colored Girls Who Want to Commit Suicide When the Rainbow is
Enough.*
We must therefore attempt to identify and describe the status of the
spoken word in cultures of heterogeneous orality such as can be found
among a number of faith communities who worship in the tradition
and style of Salem Baptist. Marshall McLuhan's pioneering study of
chirographic, typographic and oral-based cultures, and the work of
Walter Ong, prove invaluable in the effort to describe the phenomenology of orality in the context of worship.
McLuhan and Ong are the most well known among a growing
number of scholars who are examining different pre-chirographic
cultures and the typographic cultures.[13] This growing body of work
should inform any attempt to interpret traditional religious language in
the Black community. The critical factor these authors emphasize is
the radical difference in the organization and use of human senses
found in oral-based cultures.

Alphabetic and later print technology, according to McLuhan, breaks apart the perceptual sensorium of people who live in auditory-integrative cultures.

> [The] unique character of our alphabet, namely that it dissociates or abstracts not only sight and sound, but separates all meaning from the sound of the letters, save so far as the meaningless letters relate to the meaningless sounds.[14]

McLuhan describes the difference between the fragmented and integrated sensorium, and the perceptual modes they create, as "closed" and "open" respectively. Closed systems prohibit synethesia, the full interplay and integration of the senses.

> Non-literate people have...no detached point of view. They are wholly with the object. They go emphatically into it. The eye is used, not in perspective but factually, as it were. Euclidean spaces depending on much separation of sight from touch and sound are not known to them.[15]

People living within this orientation are not primarily oral, for their experience, including the experience of layering, does not appeal to a primarily singular sense; sound evokes tactility, and sight evokes olfactory ("he looks funky") as well as kinetic ("your tie is busy") perceptions. We must acknowledge that visual/typographic cultures try to achieve the same effect through verbal metaphor and symbol, for each of these literary devices is a boundary-crossing and encompassing technique. For example, "the exhibit was a visual feast" (metaphor). "The whipping post is the Puritans' maypole," which combines antithetical experience of play and punishment. The creation of a literary symbol appeals to the distended visual imagination which dominates at the expense of other senses, for "with print there is more complete separation of the visual sense from the audible-tactile."[16] On the other hand, "print technology [is] able to translate every kind of problem and experience into the more visual kind of linear order."[17] Orality invites a participatory intensity.

The synesthetic mode of being resides within a corresponding and complementary social modality described by McLuhan as "tribal." In McLuhan's usage, the term is not a pejorative, racial, geographical, religious, or genetic reference, or a particular social-ethnic organization. Tribe is a trans-historical style of existence determined by audible-tactile-visual harmonium. Language in this context is charged with the dynamics of "reasonable, live, active natural forces" in contrast to the literary culture's emphasis upon language as noetic "meaning" or "significance."[18] Language is power, event.[19]

McLuhan identifies a direct relationship between the organization and use of the human sensorium and the organization and form of social interaction. Perception and social interaction are inextricably determinative. "Tribal" is the social and perceptual mode of the synesthesic, individual and mass society belong to the dis-esthetic:

> Print is the extreme phase of alphabet culture that detribalizes or decollectivizes man in the first instance. Print raises the visual features of alphabet to highest intensity of definition, then print carries the individuating power of the phonetic alphabet much further than manuscript culture could ever do. Print is the technology of individualism.[20]

Tribal or pre-typographic communities communicate in a manner which necessitates intensive and immediate social interaction. Communication in Western literary culture depends upon ratiocentric standards of verification and logical criteria which exist independent of concrete experience. In oral communities, knowledge is socially embodied and enacted.

> The intrinsic nature of oral communication has a considerable effect upon both the content and the transmission of the cultural repertoire. In the first place, it makes for a directness of relationship between symbol and referent. There can be no reference to "dictionary definitions," nor can words accumulate the successive layers of historically validated meanings which they acquire in a literate culture. Instead the meaning of each word is ratified in a succession of concrete situations, accompanied by vocal inflexions and physical gestures, all of which combine to particularize both its specific denotation and its accepted connotative usages. This process of direct semantic ratification, of course, operates cumulatively; and as a result the totality of symbol referent relationships is more immediately experienced by the individual in an exclusively oral culture, and is thus more deeply socialized.[21]

Aside from the dualistic (sign-referent) theory of language, the insight helps us understand how oral communication depends upon as well as engenders the formation of a unique community. The community not only tests the truth; truth is something members create with one another. Set within the socially intensive environment of the tribe–oral community–language is not only expressive but bears social consequences. The spoken word creates, transforms or destroys relationships and realities. Communication in this context is inherently interactive and bodily participatory.

In addition to the interactive, socially generative character, the spoken word participates in additional dimensions of power in its ability to disclose and convey human interiority.

> True interiority makes it possible to address others: only insofar as a person has interior resources, insofar as he experiences his full self, can he also relate to Others, for addressing or relating to them involves precisely interiority, too, since they are interiors. Thus addressing others is not quite "facing" them insofar as facing is a visually-based concept that calls for a turning outward. Communication is more inwardness than outwardness. It is not entirely satisfactory even to say that man is an interior exteriorizing himself. To address or communicate with others is to participate in their inwardness as well as in our own. Sound binds interiors to one another's interiors.[22]

The power of the spoken word within community is determined by the interactive human relationships. If we now return to the sensorial organization that is characteristic of orality—the synesthetic or simultaneous interactions of the senses—people in oral cultures tend toward simultaneity of communication and being. We need to examine the way in which simultaneity of being and expression manifest themselves.

Multidimensionality of perception and existence of any examined phenomena–language, objects, subjectivity, worship, literature–is precisely the reality that phenomenology seeks to disclose and portray, for unlike the science-based empirical positivism which inevitably leads to linear, causal and therefore reductionistic explanations, phenomenology, based upon experiential empiricism and intuition, concludes that things exist only in the multidimensionality of their dependent relationships. Translating the events of worship into a text which is examined from the standpoint of linguistic considerations alone is a reduction of the experience rather than the edictic reduction to essence.

To return to our point of entry, which is phenomenology's concentration upon presence and experience, we can proceed to investigate the acoustic dimensions of presence within the setting of traditonal Black worship. Immediately we encounter the problem inherent in the very phenomenological method we hope to employ which will disclose the experience. Phenomenology, while trying to escape the difficulties of philosophical predispositions and assumptions, is rooted in a single-sense, visualist approach to the world. Ong points out that *phainomenon* (appearance) comes from *phainein* (to show, expose to sight).[23]   He reminds us that the Greek term *eidos* (idea) "is patently visual, from the same root as the term 'vision.'"[24]

Applying implicitly visualist-based modes of understanding to aural experience results in a form of sedimentation that Ihde calls "metaphor-metaphysics."[25]   The procedure is metaphorical in that the process crosses the boundaries, in this case of phenomena and perception; metaphysical in that one experience becomes the foundation of another. Even phenomenology's search for "essence" leads to an embedded visualist bias. *Esse* from *es* (to be, is) becomes the root of essence. The form appears in "presence" from the Latin *praesens*, present participle of *praeesse* (to be before one, be present: *prae-* [in front of] + *esse* [to be]).

Presence, phenomenon, *eidos*, essence, as they have evolved within phenomenology, have a decidedly visual-unidirectional ambient. Sound in general, and the gathering of voices of an oral/aural community of worship, assumes an omni-directional, multi-dimensional, and, most importantly for this study, simultaneous character.

Presence in the aural sensorium is less a place than a "standing before" or a directional line of observation. Presence as the experiential locus of phenomenological investigation is a radically redefined understanding of being *(dasein)*, and can only be answered by looking at the concrete enactments and utterances of the praying and worshipping moment.

Prayer Meeting, Deacon's Devotion, and Worship: Community, *Communitas*, and Cosmos

If we identify each of these related occasions when the body of believers gathers at Salem, we can distinguish them by the character of what is revealed, manifested, or "spoken forth" in the Heideggerian view.

> All phenomenological investigation involves the descriptive registration of founding relationships among the reflectively revealed determinators of experience.[26]

While the control and structure of the prayer meeting moves from laity to hierarchy, the gathering nonetheless remains the one place where members can present the testimony of their unique encounters with

God. Testimony is the public sharing of the individual's narrative before the community.

This narrative reveals dimensions of the members' lives which cannot enter into the deacon's devotion or the worship service. But the art of testifying is also an invitation extended to members to enter more deeply into the life of the individual through the request for performing prayers, evoked confirmation, spontaneous affirmation and empathy. The narrative disclosure of God and self not only requires a community but constitutes one. Johnson, employing Baker Brownell's definition of community, provides a working definition for our purposes:

> (a) a group of neighbors who know one another face to face; (b) a diversified group in age, sex and function; (c) a cooperative group in which the main activities of life are carried on together; (d) a group having a sense of belonging or solidarity; and (e) a rather small group in which members know one another as whole persons, not as functional fragments.[27]

In Salem's setting, one might add a further definition: a group whose members share and recognize and confirm a common experience and commitment to God.

In the prayer meeting the evidence of individual experience is told forcefully, powerfully, most often but not always by women, who stand before the other members. The interpersonal intimacy of recalling God's involvement in one's life during crisis, despondent periods, desperation, and near-fatal illness and injury are bonding moments for the members to each other and to God.

The testimony's power resides not in a simple retelling; the narration depends upon the immersion of the sister or brother in the throes of his or her struggle and appeal before God. As the testifying individual's personal dilemma with God unfolds, the power and passion of the speaker's piety is unveiled. The event is descriptive, expressive and theologically pregnant. Ong reminds us:

> Because in its physical constitution as sound, the spoken word proceeds from the human interior and manifests human beings to one another as conscious interiors, as persons, the spoken word forms human beings into close-knit groups. When a speaker is addressing an audience, the members of the audience normally become a unity with themselves and with the speakers.[28]

> The word itself is both interior and exterior: it is, as we have seen, a partial exteriorization of an interior seeking another interior.[29]

In the disclosive act which demands vulnerability before the group in portraying one's vulnerability before God, a new dimension is created, one which is not an act of narrative recall, of bringing forth past events. The testifying witness in the prayer meeting creates a present moment, a divine-social-personal moment when God acts transformatively in becoming manifest unexpectedly through His powers. The narrative act and the event recounted are not separate moments, but a new moment is created as members witness the transformation of the witness by her very act of testimony. She experiences God anew in the act, and the members confirm her truth in bold utterance, and recognize the presence of the Spirit amongst them.

To illustrate the difference between the narrated event and the moment of manifestation, we need only look at the testimony itself. In Linda Perkins' story, God's activity became manifest when she went to the mailbox.

> There was a letter from the insurance company. And I said, "Ooohhh Lord, what's wrong now?" And something told me–it was the Holy Spirit–to go in the house. So I went in the house and it said, "Open it up."

Once inside her home, she opened the letter and found an unexpected settlement check sufficient to pay her pressing debt. During her testimony, however, the moment which moved her listeners to an expressive outcry came after her reaffirmation of the commitment she made to serve God totally, without reservation, placing all of her personal resources at His disposal. In other words, at the moment she described a position of extreme dependency and vulnerability came her powerful affirmation of God's unpredictable deliverance and reliability. As her testimony moved toward the moment of power, she began to crumble, voice cracking, tears falling, then shouting her faith in God: "I'm a living witness!! He'll work it out for you!!!" This moment of personal depth disclosed in weakness revealed Linda's power, the power to be fully present, a wholeness which contains vulnerability, weakness, uncertainty, yet persistent reliance upon God even when one cannot summon the strength to endure. Upon the manifestation of Linda's power, God's power then entered into the prayer room, moving the members to affirm the truth of what they heard to signal God's unseen presence.

Linda's life had entered into the lives of the praying members, leaving an interior mark of their indelible connectedness to her and to the God who manifested Himself in His power and her weakness. Divine presence depended upon and transformed interpersonal inter-action. In the aural/oral bodily enactments of community, presence is not a purely visual manifestation, but a dilation and internalization of interiority between members.   Once again, Ong's discussionion of sound and voice is helpful.

> A presence is an interiority bearing toward and calling to another interior, an inwardness which is simultaneously an utterance or "outerance" or "outering" insofar as the other is outside.   And yet this "outering" is not merely an outwardness, not an abandonment of interiority for exteriority. The voice really goes out of me. But it calls not to something outside, but to the inwardness of another. It is a call of one interior through an exterior to another interior.[30]

The manifestation of Linda's interiority called forth in narrative is also an invitation to others to be fully present before her and God. As the testimonial act and utterance before members moves across the multiple boundaries of the past event (chronological–toward a new experience in the present moment), Linda's story and affirmation bring her to the edge of her limits, her human resources, and as she undergoes the throes of living for and depending upon the uncontrollable power of God, she enters into the same relationship of entrusting her weakness, her interiority, her vulnerability to the members of the prayer meeting.   Presence is made manifest in moments of heightened simultaneity: chronological, semantic, intersubjective and interactive presence of Afro-American worship depends upon the creation and experience of these various modes.

In testimony, the divine presence is manifested through personal narrative. But it is not the event which is re-enacted. This would place the moment in the mimetic mode of Western drama.   Rather, the sensibilities, the in-depth character and way of being with God which have been dramatized in the narrative are embodied and portrayed in a felt and deeply lived moment with the members. Presence therefore in the Afro-American modes of prayer and worship is incarnational.

Testimony in the context of the prayer meeting deepens the sense of relatedness through personal narrative disclosure and bodily affective enactment of those sensibilities of depending upon deity. Power and presence become felt through the individual in the context of receptive members, but the emphasis and locus is the particularity of the testifying person. Salem creates numerous occasions to build a sense of relatedness necessary to maintain continuity in a church of its size. The various ministers, outreach programs, choir and committees, associates, Bible study, are all communal cells in a larger body. Members bring therefore a strong sense of their belonging to the larger body and to their interior communal cells when they come to Sunday worship.

We now turn to the deacon's devotion to examine the modes of presence in terms of relationality and simultaneity.

Deacon's Devotion: Ritual of *Communitas*

Victor Turner alerts us to a dialectical relationship between structure and *communitas*.[31] The establishment of *communitas* depends upon and emerges out of structure. While structure does not always imply an arrangement of hierarchy, as we have seen at Salem and in Black society in general, hierarchy, power and privilege with its necessary sets of subordination are found throughout its various organizations. Turner, quoting Robert Merton, identifies "role-sets" as "the actions and relationships that flow from a social status."[32] Since the creation of *communitas* occurs within the periods of liminality, one must identify its threshold, keeping in mind that *communitas* depends upon the existence of community (see above).

The movement from structure to *communitas* is not as radical in the deacon's devotion as rites of passage or kinship installation. We must remember that even with the prevalence of hierarchy, Salem labors toward being a community whose members refer to it as a family. Nevertheless the deacons are the respected and presiding elders of the community, often the recipients of reverence and affection. Until recently the office was exclusively occupied by older males in their 50s and 60s. Of late the church has expanded the select to include females, awkwardly called deaconesses, and adolescents, referred to as junior deacons. They are always well attired and comport themselves with dignity, gravity of bearing and grace. They are guardians of both the church as an institution, responsible for choosing a new pastor if one should retire, expire, or depart, as well as providing oversight in the areas of finance, mission and operations. In this sense they are similar to a board of trustees responsible for the overall integrity rather than the day-to-day operations of the institution. Deacons have the additional responsibility of keeping the spiritual identity of the community kindled through counsel and the ritual of their moving devotional.

Turner points out that "lowliness and sacredness and homogeneity and comradeship"[33] are found within the creation of *communitas* during liminality. The deacon's devotion initiates this movement with the song leader antiphonally leading the entire gathering of members who answer him in a manner which is both improvised and familiar. While singing, the elders stand as the designated song leader divests himself of the visible sign of his office: the well-tailored suit coat with emblematic red handkerchief and lapel flower. His white long-sleeved shirt now stands in contrast to the suited men surrounding him. The leader now bears the sartorial mark of vulnerability. Unprotected by rank and raiment, the chosen deacon prepares to come before the Holy in a state of vulnerability and humility. As the deacon prepares to make his descent, his fellow deacons gather around him, offering tactile affirmation in hand clasps, shakes, touching his shoulders, verbally accompanying him in the midst of the members' singing. The community's entire focus rests upon this chosen man who will go before the Creator and Maker of the cosmos with the prayers gathered from and expressed for the assembled members and the entire church community.

In several respects, the moment and symbolism in the deacon's devotion are the inverse of the prayer meeting held earlier in the week. There, one member came before the body with an individual testimony or request for prayer uttered in an idiosyncratic narrative according to her particular need, experience, or encounter with God. Here, the community goes to an individual with empowering affirmation and with more general, collective prayer needs. Although the entire body has yet to arrive, the church is represented in the hierarchy of deacons. The individual personality and needs of the deacon are unimportant, even irrelevant, for the ritual gestures of affirmation and bonding create and endow him with a collective persona. While he is a man going before the awesome deity, he is Everyman as he lifts the prayers of the faithful before God. The power of his prayer does not depend upon his personal testimony, but upon his ability to evoke an atmosphere fraught with awe and gratitude.

The deacon's ritual of gestural affirmation and bonding expresses another dimension of the actions unfolding before us. Phenomenologists attempt to reveal embedded dimensions of experience by starting from a position, which does not eliminate the possibility of multiple disclosure by premature imposition of closure–theoretical, explanatory, or metaphysical. Affirmation, bonding, comradeship are all present in the preparations the deacon must undergo before praying. If we return to the act of divestment, which signals the movement from hierarchy to humility in the presence of the sacred, we can detect another dimension. The deacon's act of removing his suit coat is preparation for physically intense labor. Suits distinguish between the office worker and the manual laborer, between the "clean" work of the mind and the "dirty" work of the laborer.

Praying, for the deacon, is laboring in the Spirit. One prays in the Spirit with one's entire person, which includes the body. If we bring the dimension of physical labor in relation to the tactile gestures of affirmation, the rite of greeting and touching not only bonds and affirms, the ritual is an act of strengthening and empowerment. We must ask: why does this act of praying demand the supportive resources of one's fellow deacons and the laity? Before answering, let us broaden the focus. The hymns and spirituals sung during the deacon's devotion create an atmosphere of mournful obeisance. The deacon's musical corpus, unlike the high-energy up-tempo urban gospel music, articulates the burden of longing for God, pleading for mercy, declaring radical dependency on the divine from a condition and posture of powerlessness. These hymns express a profound commitment to God while embracing the uncertainty of suffering and death. While gospel music celebrates and enacts episodes of divine empowerment, deliverance and transformation, the content and tone of the deacon's hymns emphasize grateful dependency in the face of the uncertain and uncontrollable power of God. Even when the members sing traditional hymns such as "Amazing Grace," which describes deliverance from sin, death and damnation, the tone of the performance maintains an atmosphere of mournful reverence.

If we take as our context the acoustic resonance of mournful pleading and gratitude which sustains the deacon's service, and return to the deacon selected to pray, we recognize a correspondence between the experience worshippers bring to the service, the movements and disposition of the deacon, and the character of the deity worshipped. Members who attend the deacon's devotion bring their suffering and affliction to this service. The dimension of their experience amplified is that of suffering and mourning, which form the context of praise and thanksgiving. The painful contingencies of life—its hazards, calamities, and violence—continue to shape Black existence in this century. Each deacon who prays addresses this shared condition and common knowledge in his prayers. His verbal articulations combined with the position of his body reveal not only the conditions of the community and their attitudes toward God, but the nature of divinity as well.

Examining the content of the prayers, we discover the polyvalent perceptions of deity and the corresponding devotional attitudes. The divinity revealed in these moments is addressed as merciful, loving, wise and powerful, but hidden within these attributes are implicit references to the God who chose to visit His power upon His creation, including the righteous, in the form of natural and social disasters, violence and misfortune: the God who takes the living into the land of death.

> Thank you God, for my lying down last night,
> Thank you God, for sending down your guardian angel,
> He watched over us all night long
> While we lied down clutching to our self,

You keep the blood running warm in our veins.

The same deity who created this world can destroy it, just as He can turn the warm blood cold and end the believer's life. This ambivalent perception is found in the scriptural interpolations of the slaves. Genesis 9, which concludes the story of the flood, portrays God in the act of providing a sign, the bow (in the King James Version, which most slaves heard and which remains the standard version used in traditional Black churches). With the rainbow comes the promise never to destroy the earth again. Slaves, acknowledging the uncontrollable character of this deity and their contingent relationship with Him, parsed the story as:

> God gave Noah the rainbow sign
> No more water, the fire next time[34]

The slave spiritual restores the power of destruction to the God of creation, maintaining the complex unresolved features of His nature. Destruction and death are inextricably linked aspects of Black existence and conceptions of deity. Nate Shaw expresses the same complex sensibility in the transcription of his life story, *All God's Dangers*. The title comes from a part of his testimony: "All God's dangers ain't a white man." The crucial point is that both the dangers and blessings belong ultimately to Him.

The deacon who prepares to pray, therefore, brings to the moment the experience and knowledge, both personal and collective, of the uncertainties which inform the shared condition of the believer's life and the behavior of the divinity. The deacon's act of removing his jacket, kneeling, and praying enacts this knowledge and reveals the multifaceted nature of this God. The act of kneeling before the rude metal folding chair embodies human frailty and desperation, while also pointing toward a deity whose power is beyond of the control of the believers. The deacon's posture reveals the host of related sensibilities and affections necessary to the act of prayer if it is to be efficacious: yielding, relinquishing, personal abandon, submission, servanthood, humility, capitulation.

Unlike the Wednesday night prayer meeting and the church service (that follows the deacon's devotion), the deacons' service does not anticipate the sudden outbreak and demonstration of God's power. The fact that anyone ambulatory, breathing, sane, as traditional prayers attest, is sufficient demonstration of beneficent power. Nevertheless, the deacon's approach to the naked metal chair has a peculiar quality, for the site that it demarcates is occupied by the unseen Creator (and Destroyer) of the universe. The power surrounding and occupying this position is both latent and evident. In the understanding of the gathered believers, the chair is the foot of the cross, the foot of God's celestial and cosmic throne. At this place and at any moment, God can execute judgment and claim the life that He has imparted to every believer and non-believer, sinner and saint. The chair stands alone and vacant, thereby creating a sense of both presence and absence. Presence in that the chair occupies space and is an object which commands attention; absence in that its outline anticipates the shape of the human body while designating the site of the unseen deity. This site is therefore the same place where Jesus was/is crucified, where the judgment of God was/is executed upon all sinful creatures. The cross reaches into the domain of heaven from which God's throne extends to earth. The site is one of multivalent convergence: sacred time, past and present, Jesus once crucified and being crucified; sacred space: Golgotha, Palestine and the sanctuary of Salem Baptist in Atlanta; cosmology: heaven and earth; soteriological site: judgment and grace; existential: life and death; affective: dread and gratitude.

This catalog of convergences, however, does not exhaust or account for the ineffable atmosphere evoked in members during the service. God is present but not completely manifest, for this dimension of deity remains remote and unincarnated. This God is not a friend, partner, or brother, terms used to describe Jesus. This deity resists all attempts at familial domestication. One hears reference to "the Spirit" during the devotion, but the term does not pertain to the God who is implored from the foot of the cross. The Spirit is manifest by the degree of participation and involvement of the members during the song chants, as measured by the quality of mourning and anguish in their voices. The power which is implored and for which one is thankful does not send members into kinetic animation or the crisis of possession. Ecstatic power is visited upon those during the worship service proper. Here the emphasis is upon proximity of human need, suffering and thanksgiving in relationship to the present yet remote, and as yet not fully demonstrated powers of this cosmic God. The center of His power remains within His realm and must be approached with fear and trembling.

One can recognize some of the characteristics of the *mysterium tremendum* and *mysterium fascinans* described by Otto.[35] The wholly other quality of God makes God the locus of power which can only be indirectly designated but not embodied or incarnated. This divinity levels distinctions between people for all power is ultimately held within Him. The response engendered by this shared experience brings the community together during this liminal period. The members' association of death and sacrality creates strong feelings of dependency upon God and each other.

Perhaps this is why the attempts made by Salem's hierarchy to introduce gender equality by incorporating women into the office and function of the deacons seems awkward, ineffectual, ritually inefficacious. On the few occasions when women (awkwardly called deaconesses: since Biblical Greek does not differentiate between male and female deacons, the term "deacon" is inclusive) pray with their male counterparts, the results are disruptive and, according to many members, unsatisfactory. One occasion is illustrative. As the song leader lined the hymn, the males stood and approached the woman elected to pray. The traditional act of removing the jacket did not take place, thus eliminating one of the crucial gestures which signal the movement into liminal *communitas*. Another deacon lowered the microphone to chair level, where the deacons' prayers are amplified over the house P.A. system. When the moment arrived for the prayer, the woman spoke from a standing position, leaving the chair unoccupied, and her voice inaudible to many in the back pews. Her prayer broke the traditional pattern established by the males. Instead of pleading, imploring, she exhorted, narrated, attested to the powerful workings of God in her life; in short, she testified. This posture and utterance belongs to a different mode, designed to reveal the visitation of deity. Women stand to testify. Turning to address the congregation alters the focus and changes the ambiance. She becomes the point of entry through which power emanates. Her testimony speaks of God's demonstrated power, rather than serving as a reminder of His past mercy.

The failure of this new rite is due not to the fact that she and other women fail to follow the established set of gestures and movements. If she had, the results would still be ineffective. A woman removing an article of clothing in public is not equivalent to a male's performance of the same action. When a man divests himself of his suit jacket, labor and vulnerability are evoked. When a woman performs the same gesture, seduction is evoked. These culturally determined perceptions of women interrupt the male movement from hierarchy to humility, and deflect the intended meanings of the act.

Liminality depends upon reversals. A man becoming powerless and dependent unseats the mundane order of autonomy and culturally prescribed definitions of masculinity. Women are located in positions of relative powerlessness, through roles associated with procreation, servitude, submission, dependency. For a woman to remove an article of clothing and kneel before the company of male deacons does not undo, but rather reinforces the normative order of power, role and function. In other words, the woman re-introduces structure in the context of anti-structure, shattering the conditions of *communitas*.

Within the context of the prayer meeting, however, the actions of women take on a different meaning. When women stand, face the congregation, and speak out of a condition of desperation at the extreme limit of endurance, while testifying to the actions of God, they invoke and release a power that transforms their condition and status. Testifying moves them from powerlessness to empowerment, reversing the social position.

Power distinguishes members. The latent power of the deity whose holiness is affirmed and recognized in mourning and supplication makes all members equal. It should be noted that in this state of pleading and supplication, the members send forth a solitary figure who prays for them all. But before doing so, they affirm the relational ties with this figure, and act in unison as one body, first by singing, then by standing as a group immediately before the deacon descends to the mercy seat. Who is this deity that requires members to undergo rituals of bonding, affirmation and receptive humility, in other words, to a community, before being able to approach Him alone?

Thus far we have examined two modes of presence in the context of communal bonding, which evoke bodily and verbal articulation. In the first act of testifying, recalling and conveying personal exploits and afflictions of one's recent past, and the activities of a merciful God, one initiates the activity of the Holy Spirit in the present. "I talked myself happy" or "I done got happy sharing my witness" are cultural expressions of the sudden and unexpected visitation of power. Personal disclosure makes one the manifest site of divine power whose presence is witnessed and confirmed in community. Presence emerges from the depth's of one's interiority in sound and gesture, connecting all who are gathered to the past and present moment of the testifying member's life, creating a unitary experience. The act of personal disclosure becomes an event of divine disclosure, inviting members into a deeper participation and relationship with the individual standing before them.

The deacon's devotion endeavors to create *communitas* by abolishing individual distinctions. Personal testimony recedes, collective concerns emerge, articulated by a representative of the community who is endowed with a communal persona. The dimensions of deity are made present by the absence of the act or event of demonstrable power. The hymns which are offered forth by the members and prayers of the various deacons are emotionally sculpted outlines of God whose power and greatness are ineluctable. He is approached with reminders of His past activity and supplications for the future, but the present manifestation of power remains concealed, formless and remote.

Congregational Worship:
From Community to *Communitas* to Cosmos

Summarizing the preceding investigation into the phenomenology of presence within the prayer meeting and deacon's devotion, the eidetic reduction of each mode may be described as follows.

Within the prayer meeting, presence is narratively invoked by a single witness whose oral account before the body of believers enables divine presence to erupt into the moment. The essence of the ritually stylized oral narrative, known in the vernacular as testifying, roots the divine presence in the experience of sacred time, God's time. The cultural and historical sedimentations are embedded in the performative act and the response: "He may not be there when you want Him but He's always right on time." "I am a time God." "You don't know what time it is." "What time is it?" "How long?" "Not long" The narrative act creates the ground for the possibility of the eruptive moment of divine-personal disclosure, creating a deeper experience of community or common recognition of a shared experience, both past and present.

Within the deacon's devotion, conventional time recedes in the consciousness of participants. The moment is suspended in timelessness, theologically identified as eternity, the time which deity inhabits. Presence, therefore, depends less upon time than place. Presence is spatially designated by the rude metal chair, the kneeling deacon, the absent visible manifestation of inexorable deity. The ritualized preparations which precede the entrance into the demarcated sacral site are also the commencement of *communitas*. The primary interactive realm is found between the deacons who enact the postures, sensibilities, feeling and gestures necessary to approach the sacred realm. The laity provides increasing support and affirmation expressed in collective acts of gestures of rising, sitting, singing. Approaching the sacred requires the enactment of supportive community.

The worship service proper, or congregational worship, builds upon the experiences of community and *communitas* which members bring to and create within the Sunday worship. Worship begins by establishing a general sense of community, which eventually moves toward an enlarged *communitas*, and results in the experience of cosmos. Presence, which has been experienced as singular (as in testifying) and centralized (in the designated site of the deacon's devotion), will become omnipresent. Worship, therefore, can be understood as the experience of the movement of sacred presence from centralized sites to diffuse, multiple and unpredictably explosive visitations of the Spirit. This movement is inseparable from the heightened sense of simultaneous activity which addresses and calls forth the response of the total personal sensorium and intensive communal interaction.

The transition from the deacon's devotion to the congregational worship is neither abrupt nor demarcated. Members have been arriving and taking their usual seats throughout the service. While they maintain their distance, filling the remote pews first, the growing crowd slowly diminishes the distance until the original participants in the deacon's devotion are no longer part of a distinct group. The entire nave responds with sounds and rhythmic prayers. Into the mournful intensity of the service, the organist sounds chords of a brighter timbre. The voice of an electric instrument, modern, upbeat and amplified, alerts the congregation that another phrase of worship is about to begin. The deacon's devotion closes in the midst of the transitional activity when one of the deacons approaches the metal chair, marking the footstool of the throne of God, folds it up, and places it in the back room to the left of the chancel. His movements are unrehearsed, unceremonial, and unnoticed by the congregants, whose attention is directed toward a number of different activities, until Rev. Sypho ascends to the pulpit and leads the congregation in an opening hymn.

Does the carefully created *communitas* dissipate with congregational worship? In a formal sense, yes. Each deacon resumes conventional dress and occupies the first pew of each section, forming a semi-circle in front of the chancel. The ushers and nurses are at their stations, executing their appointed task and fulfilling their roles as officers in a larger multi-staffed ministry. Mission Society members are in white uniforms. The choir is about to process to music created by competent, professional musicians. All of the visible signs of the structure are in place, as a new order and style of worship begins. We must note, however, that the intensity of the deacon's prayers and the members' singing is such that the atmosphere of communal, rather than personal, intimacy created through the bonding rituals of people deeply aware of the threat of death and the uncontrollable power of God remains in the consciousness of even those who only observe the rite. The knowledge and experience of the ultimate contingency of existence, a contingency that is not eliminated by God, but rather resides within Him, makes a profoundly fundamental claim upon the diverse members. The truth of Black life which upward economic mobility cannot eliminate is the fact that members of the Black community have yet to develop an identity which is legitimated institutionally and supported in the prevailing culture. In other words, they occupy no place of uncontested authority or personhood. Even when they have yet to encounter the Creator of the universe in a near-death experience as many of the deacons and elderly members have, they are nonetheless never free of the impingements of finitude. This knowledge is ritually reawakened, enacted and confirmed in the deacon's devotion.

The reestablishment of structure, therefore, allows for a residual presence of *communitas* as the worship service begins. The sense of communality as noted above is emphasized and reinforced by congregational singing, study, and sitting as one body reciting the Lord's prayer. Even Rev. Sypho, who initiates the first song, sings with the congregation. All of these activities continue to build upon and nourish the experience of being one body, a community at worship.

The crucial importance of these actions becomes clear when we note at what point the pastor enters the pulpit. Pastor Williams does not appear until activities sufficient to create a sense of belonging and involvement, in essence communality, within the congregation have been completed. The engagement of the members' attention, the heightened interactive response with the choir, instrumentalists, deacons and laity is not only necessary to what he hopes to accomplish, but fundamental to traditional Black worshippers' experience of the sacred.

One need only compare this context to the Roman Catholic rite, where the celebration begins with the entrance of the priest and ends with his recession. The presence of the priest, both a member and representative of the hierarchy, constitutes the community. He manifests the power and controls the focus of the Eucharistic presence. Within the Afro-Christian context of Salem Baptist, the pastor's entrance depends *a priori* upon the communal; the cohesiveness and interactive unity must be well under way before the pastor can continue and complete the transformation. Transformation is common to both rituals; their telos and focus, however, distinguish them. The Catholic rite seeks primarily transformation of the sacramental object, and the relationship of the congregants to its presence. Afro-Christian worship seeks to transform the matrix of communal relationship. The work of Afro-Christian liturgy is the evocation of the community's response to its deepest afflictions and gravest injuries along with the invocation of the wounded presence of Jesus. The simultaneous manifestation creates the conditions for the transformation of the community's suffering and the shared experience of a compassionate cosmos.

The shifts in tone, tense, rhythm and bodily gesture at different points in the worship all engender and invite greater affective, noetic and bodily participation. The emphasis upon simultaneity which makes all events interconnected begins to create a global sense of divine presence which anyone who has ever visited or participated in the service cannot help but notice and feel. One is surrounded by a field of electric, unpredictable energy.

In the course of the service, the members are conducted through several different presentations or episodes of religious life, which in effect create different frames. The pastor controls the pace and moment of each frame, providing enormous latitude within the individual moments. For example, the pastor can transform the ritual of hospitality into an opportunity to address political issues, or celebrate a homecoming, or affirm the importance of family ties, depending on the visitors and the mood of the moment. The Scripture lesson can include sermonettes, which are complete works in miniature. Musicians and choir can exercise similar flexibility. For example, the choir usually performs a slower, reflective selection during the period immediately before the Scripture lesson. The music serves as both transition and preparation for the formal examinations of God's word. If the music moves members to a greater degree of interaction, the choir and musicians can either continue to sustain the members' state or facilitate its conclusion. The worshippers' frame is altered and diverse feelings and aspects of the believer's life are called forth–humor, hurt, reverence, despondency, dejection, deliverance and joy–until the entire ensemble of religious emotions has been touched.

The service communicates to worshippers that this is a safe place to be vulnerable and expressive. The cumulative effect is the collapsing of boundaries and the creation of a new unity. Eventually, Pastor Williams not only evokes but enacts these affections and postures.

If the multiple foci of worship work effectively, the members not only move closer to one another as a group, they have allowed their real and complex emotional terrain to be touched and shaped by song, rhythm, drama and word. Community in worship is both an interpersonal and inter-subjective creation. The second turn toward *communitas* takes place after the calling forth of the congregation's affective interiority.

Liturgy and *communitas* begin not with visual, but with vocal signals. Whooping, as described previously, is the technique utilized by the pastor to call forth and act out the community's collective feeling, experience, understanding of Jesus. The pastor becomes the singular presentation of the interactive communal experience of deity. He therefore labors to simulate and effect the simultaneity found with the rhythms of the instrumentalists, the call and response of the choir and solo, the testifying responsive confirmative relationship between witness and members.

The fundamental movement in the pastor's performance is the shift from his private persona to the creation of a communally recognizable character of Jesus. The pastor recedes; Jesus's presence enlarges. Verb tenses change from past to present tense: "I believe I can see Jesus now, by the boats on the lake." The rhythmic, percussive, gutteral utterances suspend time, for they return to and maintain a syncopated pattern punctuating the improvised Gospel narrative. If the preceding stages of worship have engaged the total sensorium and generated a heightened sense of community, then the pastor is being heard and seen in a manner which enables his motions, meter and oratory to create a new dimension of presence which McLuhan describes as the synesthetic reception of spoken words, as one of "total interdependence and interrelation," a "resounding world of simultaneous relations of oral and acoustic space."[36]

> For until literary culture deprives language of this multidimensional resource, every word is a poetic world unto itself, a momentary deity or revelation, as it seemed to non-literal man.[37]

Words in their aural-somatic social matrix possess the divine power of simultaneous multiplicity. The spoken word generates multidimensionality of affect, i.e. presence. Ong echoes McLuhan's insight:

> Because it situates me in the midst of a world, sound conveys simultaneity. Although sound itself is fleeting, as we have seen, what it conveys at any instant of its duration is not dissected but caught in the actuality of the present, which is rich, manifold, full of diverse action, the only moment when everything is really going on at once.[38]

The transition from community to *communitas* is also a fundamental movement from language as reference, i.e. language understood primarily as referential signs and symbols, to an experience of language as presence. Symbols generate simultaneous reference to multiple realms of meaning. The spoken word under these conditions becomes the multidimensionality of presence. "Auditory synthesis overwhelms me with phenomena beyond all control."[39]

Presentational (as opposed to referential) modes mark the entrance into the cosmic ultimacy of the suffering, crucified and risen Jesus. Since the traditional methodology of liturgical studies focuses exclusive attention to the text, we will attempt to disentangle the experience from referential-semantic subversion.

Cassirer provides one account in terms of Darwinian evolution, Kantian dialectical linguistics. Beginning with a Kantian-influenced perspective of bifurcated noema/noetic phenomena, Cassirer envisioned a primitive era of linguistic experience of fusion between symbol and referent.[40] While his theories are fecund, they raise issues which are beyond the scope of this project. I have found the thinking of Robert Plant Armstrong to be far more helpful and congruent with the material under consideration.[41]

Armstrong's study of West African art and literature in particular, and culture in general, utilizes a phenomenology of aesthetics. Although the following statement describes the experience of African objects of art, the conclusions are applicable to the experience of language with in an oral-communal context.

> One cannot say that the affecting presence is a symbol referring as it were to itself, for this is not what a symbol does, and this one can no more say that an affecting presence is a symbol of itself than I can say of any person that he is a symbol of himself. The affecting object, on the other hand, the host in the mass–does refer to something external to itself; therefore, it is a symbol.[42]

One can argue from the stance of a devoted Catholic believer who partakes of the host that the Eucharist encompasses symbolic dimensions, but becomes an exceptional category of symbol, transparent in Paul Tillich's description, i.e. the bread *is* the body of Christ. But the referential quality is maintained by the designation of the host as the sacramental body of Christ. Although the term carries theological weight and may be prematurely introduced at this point in the discussion, Armstrong uses the word "incarnation" to distinguish the referential externalization of sign/referent dichotomies.

> The enactment, the incarnation which is the affecting presence, is directly perceived as and for what it is, and what it is inextricably affecting...The affecting presence is thus a presentational presence, and it is existentially "all there."[43]

In other words, Armstrong's analysis enables us to break the Platonic paradigm (or metaphoric metaphysic) which bifurcates reality and language as mimetic and referential, i.e. that language refers to a reality "out there" or somewhere removed from the locus of utterance. The members of Salem experience words spoken and enacted in worship not as reference or symbol, but in the multidimensionality of *presence*.

The manifestation of presence within communities of worship is understood by members as "Spirit." The achievement of Pastor Williams' "whooping" alters mundane time into sacred time, which does not move in linear progression but maintains liminal suspension. Participants experience an increase in the affective, kinetic possibilities in the midst of a high religious drama. The pastor, in other words, "calls down the Spirit." Members describe this experience as a pervasive sensation which is both specifically localized and yet encompasses the entire community. The response to this moment is never predictable or singular. One can observe wide-ranging reactions. One woman rocks in time to the percussive, gutteral ensemble of the pastor's whooping back-beat. A man next to her moves to the edge of his pew, inclining, intently focussed upon the pastor. Another woman is in tears, quietly intoning "Jesus" with thanksgiving. A man shouts "Thank You Jesus" in an explosion of joy becoming hilarity. Multiple affective possibilities are being called forth, and the expression of one does not eliminate the appearance of others.

As the worship intensifies, Pastor Williams is no longer the central focus or locus of activity. Interaction with him is initiated from any of the various sites, choir, deacons, etc. At the same time, decentralized, non-interactive behavior emerges. An elderly woman races up and down the aisle; she is oblivious to all. A middle-aged woman loses consciousness in her pew. An exhaustive inventory of various activities and behaviors during the "whooping" period of the sermon has yet to be compiled.

The behavior which has attracted the greatest attention among professional students and voyeurs are the incidents of spirit possession. The common orientation which shapes these studies is the assumption that spirit possession is the consummation of the believers' liturgical expectations, and therefore the center of worship and an ultimate experience.[44]

Given the frenzied kinetic behavior exhibited by members during the crisis of possession, and the position of importance this experience has occupied within indigenous West African and African diasporic cults, the emphasis and conclusion are justifiable. Within the worship and community of Salem, however, both expectations and the response to spirit possession differ from these normative definitions.

During the interviews that I conducted over a period of eighteen months, none of the members ever stated that they attended services with the expectation of seeing others or themselves "possessed" by the Spirit. When asked what was the most important experience in worship, the majority answered "feeling the Spirit" or "knowing Jesus was there." None of the members who actually experienced possession anticipated the event, nor did they feel disappointed or lacking when they were not the host of the visitation. Given the modern heterogeneous composition of Salem's community, when members encompass the social, economic, educational and religious spectrum, we need to reinterpret the meaning of worship and the role of spirit possession, especially in those traditions which were shaped by the oppressive conditions of chattel slavery.

As an alternative interpretation of the expectations and experience of worship, I propose that during the period defined by the pastor's technique of whooping, members experience an intense and sustained moment of synesthetic integration and interpersonal connectivity wherein the conventional boundaries between emotions, persons, and social roles collapse to create a global experience of ultimate and transcendent order, i.e. cosmos. In the Black vernacular, "everything is everything!" Wholeness for the traditional Black American believer includes rather than excludes chaos. Like the African musicians who hear the rattle of the mbira gourd as part of the music, or the squeaks and breath rattles of Coltrane or the screams of Pharoah Sanders, all of these elements have a necessary place in the spectrum.

The crisis of possession belongs as much to the community as it does to the individual. Rather than seeing the members of Salem who undergo the throes of ecstatic possession as individuals who have entered the climax of worship, they may be better understood as members who have experienced the collapse of all boundaries of pain and pleasure, individual and community, human and deity. The integration of all realms which constitute the individual becomes explosively manifest in the ecstatic moment, and her identity becomes obscured in the embodiment of this New World African deity called Jesus, called Holy Ghost–the One known only in and through ultimate interrelatedness. The church member in ecstasy has become divine communality incarnate: known intimately in God's convulsive visitation. The dreaded deity of creation and destruction, life and death, mercy and wrath to whom the deacons submitted themselves in praise, supplication and mournful humility, this unpredictable creator of the cosmos has become manifest in the individual.

The movement of the congregation's worship is inverse to the deacon's devotion. The God of life and death to whom prayers of thanksgiving and supplication are offered, but who remains remote and stationary, is not manifest in unpredictable explosions of healing power throughout the sanctuary. We might therefore understand the deacon's worship as a primary and primal enactment–almost rehearsal in dramatic terminology–of the postures, positions, attitudes, sensibilities, the ethos of vulnerability and receptivity one needs to cultivate in order to receive the manifestations of the spirit. The pastor recapitulates the deacon's posture during the height of his whooping period where he confesses his contingent existence: "I could have been dead, buried in my grave," and positions himself bodily as a dependent of the divine. The action dissociates him from the persona of Jesus he has created through the whooping narrative.

The power which erupted in the testimony of an individual believer, and whose site was designated by the rude chair and prayer, fills the entire sanctuary, bathed in beneficent healing. By cosmos, I simply mean a comprehensive ultimate order. During these moments one feels a visceral sense of belonging to everyone present. This design is not a diagram or schema, but is personally and collectively felt and internalized. This permeating power binds personal wounds and joins person to person in an experience of wholeness. The transformation of injury and alienation, pain and despair, desperation and helplessness which mark the lives of relatively powerless, marginal Black people remains at the heart of this cosmos. In the traditional Afro-Christian cosmology, as in the many African religions, conflict and chaos are included rather than excluded from the inception. Worship in this tradition allows the chaos of racism, relational rupture, and violence to be carried into the sanctuary, made corporally manifest, shared and bodily claimed by others who labor in the task of integrating its destruction into the presence and identity of a suffering deity, Jesus.

Conclusion:
Beginning of Black Phenomenological Theology

...Since the high Middle Ages with the advent of the university and of scientific methods, we have become accustomed to the notion that theology is something done in academies out of books by elites with degrees producing theologies of this and that. To argue with minds accustomed to thinking of theology in such a manner–that theology at its genesis is *communitarian*, even *proletarian*; that it is aboriginally liturgical in context, partly conscious and partly unconscious, that it stems from an experience of near chaos; that it is long-term and dialectical; and that its agents are more likely to be charwomen and shopkeepers than pontiffs and professors–all this is to argue against the grain. Aiden Kavanagh, *On Liturgical Theology*

We have come to an end and a beginning, for only upon completing the descriptive and hermeneutical task of first phenomenology are we able to provide the pointed entry for theological interpretation. This is not to suggest that the end of this monograph exhausts the possibilities of descriptive phenomenology. Dynamics of musical performance, description of thematic services (pastor's birthday, Easter, and the high holy day in Black worship, Mother's Day) could provide further material and lend additional depth to the investigation. This study has only begun to provide a broad sounding of understanding of the trimodal experience of presence within Black worship. In three settings of the prayer meeting, deacon's devotion, and congregational worship, and the corresponding modes of community, *communitas* and cosmos are edetic reductions and not intended to correspond with theologically triune understandings of deity.   Any systematic correspondence at this point would be antithetical to the phenomenological method employed throughout.

The correspondence which could provide the architecture of organic theology emerging from the experience of worship can be located within the convergence of first (primary) phenomenology, phenomenological theology, and liturgical theology.   The first phenomenological nexus has been described.

If phenomenology struggles to expose the basic relationships within the determinative elements of experience, the logical theological correlation is found within phenomenological theology which "interprets God as positively related to, even given, in religious experience and that grounds transcendental method in this larger, concretely historical view of experience."[45]

Phenomenological theology and Afro-Christian worship are empirically founded.   Within the Afro-Christian tradition, one's knowledge of God depends upon one's experience of God, an experience confirmed, validated and celebrated in worship and, as I have tried to demonstrate, experienced anew within community.   Urban Holms once noted that "good liturgy borders on the vulgar."[46]   By "vulgar" I am certain that Holms meant to imply both "belonging to the people" and "profane." Liturgy, true liturgy, involves all of one's body, sweating, muscular, fleshly, laboring, passion-filled, fearful, doubting, empty, pain-riddled, affectionate, afflicted, even sinful self.   Silence and stillness are sacraments of the Spirit's absence in the Black Church, the condemnation reserved for the inauthentic, the insincere.   In this sense, Black worship labors to include those elements considered inappropriate, undesirable, intolerable and disturbing to mainstream Euro-American Catholic and Protestant Christianity.   One need only observe the sanctuary and the service of a representative church from the latter tradition to conclude that pain, injury, the scandalous contortions of bodily suffering, and the spontaneous riot of laughter, are denied expression and privately contained.

Kavanagh stresses that liturgical theology is not simply one more species of theology, but the genesis of theology.   Worship is an event, which if authentic does something to the participants.   In this sense worship disrupts, intrudes and in the experience of those who are divinely possesses, violates, and invades the believer.   The movement toward chaos in the order of worship induces change and growth, according to Kavanagh.

> For what emerges most directly from an assembly's liturgical act is not a new species of theology among others. It is *theologia* itself.[47]

This is properly identified as *theologia prima*. In light of the much publicized advent of modern Black theology as a theology uniquely by and for Black people, which addresses a unique experience in unique ways, the majority of its practitioners employ a relatively safe, well established method of *theologia secunda*, a second theology as the theology of the academy, of the elite. Even when they take the religious experience of the slaves and contemporary Black Christians seriously, they prematurely impose categories derived from the modern, liberal, intellectual tradition upon the data.

Cone and Wilmore, the founding fathers of this approach, contend that Black Christians in particular, and Black religion in general, are most authentic when they defy, confront and struggle violently against the various structures of oppression.[48] While this form of polemical theology has its place in the academy, it has more in common with the theological practices and traditions that it criticizes as oppressive, for both Euro-American theology and contemporary Black theology valorize rhetorics of power.

The experience brought to and engendered within Black worship is one of suffering vulnerability. Power is understood and celebrated as the capacity to immerse oneself in the radical vulnerability of God, a form of sacred vulnerability where one submits to the calamitous claim of God upon one's life in a totality of surrender. When the community submits to this claim, however, a power and presence raises up, expands and encompasses the assembly, which shapes perception and reveals the cosmic designs of God's purpose. This power and presence resituates the ultimacy of oppressive structures and transforms the injury inflicted and suffering sustained into wholeness and healing. The scandalous paradox awaiting theological examination is the Black Christian experience of wholeness in the midst of violent structures of oppression.

Phenomenology provides one set of resources for describing and interpreting the various experiences cultivated in worship. Its emphasis upon the multidimensionality of experience and presence are essential to understanding worship within the oral/aural sensorium still extant in contemporary Black society. Traditional Black culture remains committed to the aesthetics of simultaneity. This fundamental intentionality in Black performance can be located in several areas: percussive polyrhythms, polydiatonicism of Coltrane, polyplanality in Bearden, rhetoric ("that was bad," "the cat was down cold"), and dance. Every African dance song

> aims at controlling not only the movement of the feet but also the movement of the toes, knees, hips, stomach, neck, head, eyes, hands,

and fingers. Each of these parts moves independently of others, yet simultaneously.[49]

This complex range of intentionality is only possible for the human sensorium under the influence of synestheia.   Even in its secular applications, the sensibility remains profoundly religious: a quest for wholeness, wholeness experienced at every level and dimension of the human being, wholeness which includes and embraces those elements that threaten existence. This is the holy inebriation of the mystics, the divine madness of the Hasidim, the improvisational ecstasy of Coltrane's extended solos, Bach's fugal majesty, Van Gogh's "Starry Night."

> Presence in the full sense of the term entails more than sensation. Insofar as it is grounded in the senses, it appears to be grounded in all of them simultaneously.[50]

Wholeness is the experience of all of one's tension-wrought dimensions like the multiple surface of African sculpture, angular and rotund, resonating as one in all its vibrant, contrary but non-contradictory possibilities. Within the exploration of this unique integration of forces, bodily articulation, and creative interaction with the divine presence in community, the distinct project of New World African-American theology begins.

Notes

Chapter 1: Introduction

1. William G. Doty, *Mythography: The Study of Myths and Rituals* (Tuscaloosa: University of Alabama Press, 1991), p. 96.

2. Ronald L. Grimes, *Beginnings in Ritual Studies* (Washington, D.C.: University Press of America, 1982), p. 43.

3. Herbert Spielberg, *Doing Phenomenology: Essays On and In Phenomenology* (The Hague: Martinus Nijhoff, 1975), p. 57.

4. Don Ihde, *Listening and Voice: A Phenomenology of Sound* (Athens: Ohio University Press, 1976), p. 18.

5. The term "electronic church" describes a group of believers, which does not exist as a true fellowship or body since they are a television and radio audience without face to face contact. They are related to the evangelist who works only through electronic media.

6. Walter Pitt, "Keep the Fire Burnin': Language and Ritual in the Afro-Baptist Church," *Journal of the American Academy of Religion* 56, no. 1 (1988): 78. This article also appears in *American Ethnologist* 16 (May 1989).

7. Melvin D. Williams, *Community in a Black Pentecostal Church: An Anthropological Study* (Prospect Heights, IL: Waveland Press, 1984), pp. 157-158.

Chapter 2: Wednesday Night Prayer Meetings

1. To cite two of numerous examples, James Baldwin's *Go Tell It On The Mountain* and composer Charles Mingus' *Wednesday Evening Prayer Meeting*.

2. James H. Cone, "Black Theology and Black Women," introductory essay in *Black Theology: A Documentary History, 1966-1979*, eds. Gayraud S. Wilmore and James H. Cone (Maryknoll, NY: Orbis Books, 1979), p. 363.

3. "Elijah;" Mahalia Jackson's version is an outstanding example.

4. Even though the eighteenth century composer John Newton and his peculiar biography are unknown to most members, the hymn has become part of the vocabulary of faith in Black churches.

5. This wondrously fragile and indispensable moment is brilliantly described in fiction by Toni Morrison in *Beloved* (New York: New American Library, Penguin Books, 1988), pp. 87-88. The character Baby Suggs, holy, is the "uncalled, unrobed, unanointed...unchurched preacher" or lay leader who facilitates the creation of the nascent community of ex-slaves by creating *communitas* in liminal space.

> When warm weather came, Baby Suggs, holy, followed by every black man, woman and child who could make it through, took her great heart to the Clearing—a wide-open place cut deep in the woods nobody knew for what at the end of a path known only to deer and whoever cleared the land in the first place. In the heat of every Saturday afternoon, she sat in the clearing while the people waited among the trees.
>
> After situating herself on a huge flat-sided rock, Baby Suggs [holy] bowed her head and prayed silently. The company watched her from the trees. They knew she was ready when she put her stick down. Then she shouted, "Let the children come!" and they ran from the trees toward her.
>
> "Let your mothers hear you laugh," she told them, and the woods rang. The adults looked on and could not help smiling.
>
> Then "Let the grown men come," she shouted. They stepped out one by one from among the ringing trees.
>
> "Let your wives and children see you dance," she told them, and the groundlife shuddered under their feet.
>
> Finally she called the women to her. "Cry," she told them. "For the living and the dead. Just cry." And without covering their eyes the women let loose..

In the character of Baby Suggs, Morrison has accurately described the antecedent to the Black Church mother, an unordained office but a vital role which has endured into the contemporary church.

6   Albert J. Raboteau, *Slave Religion* (New York: Oxford University Press, 1980), pp. 250-251.

Chapter 3: Sunday Worship Service

1. Rudolf Otto, *The Idea of the Holy: An Inquiry into the Non-Rational Factor in the Idea of the Divine and its Relation to the Rational* (London: Oxford University Press, 1924), p. 73.

2. Evan M. Zeuss, *Ritual Cosmos: The Sanctification of life in African Religions* (Athens, Ohio: Ohio University Press, 1987).

3. Salem Baptist Church Bulletin, December 3, 1989, *The Names of Our Lord*: "Jesus" Matthew 1.18-21; "Immanuel" Matthew 1.22-23; "Christ the Lord" Luke 2.10-12; and "Nazarene" Matthew 2.21-23.

Chapter 4: Phenomenological Interpretation

1. Paul Tillich, *Systematic Theology*, vol. 1 (Chicago: University of Chicago Press, 1983), p. 118.

2. Herbert Spiegelberg, *Doing Phenomenology: Essays on and in Phenomenology* (The Hague, Netherlands:Martinus Nijhoff, 1975), pp. 10, 15.

3. Don Ihde, *Listening and Voice: A Phenomenology of Sound* (Athens, Ohio: Ohio University Press, 1986), p. 17.

4. Ihde, p. 20.

5. Ihde, p. 26.

6. Ihde, p. 18.

7. Ihde, p. 18.

8. Ihde, p. 20.

9. Ihde, p. 20.

10. Ihde, p. 29.

11. Kevin Hart, *The Trespass of the Sign* (Cambridge: Cambridge University Press, 1991), p. 25.

12. Kurt Mueller-Vollmer, *The Hermeneutics Reader: Texts of the German Tradition from the Enlightenment to the Present* (New York: Continuum, 1989), p. 20.

13. Other scholars in this number include Jack Goody, *The Domestication of the Savage Mind* (Cambridge: Cambridge University Press, 1977); *The Interface Between the Written and the Oral* (Cambridge: Cambridge University Press, 1987); *The Logic of Writing and the Organization of Society* (Cambridge: Cambridge University Press, 1986); and Eric A. Havelock, *The Literate Revolution in Greece and Its Cultural Consequences* (Princeton, NJ: Princeton University Press, 1982).

14. Marshall McLuhan, *The Gutenberg Galaxy: The Making of Typographic Man* (Toronto: University of Toronto Press, 1962), p. 47.

15. McLuhan, *The Gutenberg Galaxy*, p. 37.

16. McLuhan, p. 93

17. McLuhan, p. 146.

18. J.C. Carothers in McLuhan, p. 19.

19. Cf. *dabar* in Ong, *The Presence of the Word* (Minneapolis: University of Minnesota Press, 1967), pp. 12-13.

20. McLuhan, *The Gutenberg Galaxy*, p. 158.

21. Jack Goody and Ian Watt, "The Consequences of Literacy," *Comparative Studies in Society and History* 5, no. 3 (1963): 306.

22. Ong, *The Presence of the Word*, p. 125.

23. Ong, *The Presence of the Word*, p. 74.

24. Walter T. Ong, *Interfaces of the Word: Studies in the Evolution of Consciousness and Culture* (Ithaca, NY: Cornell University Press, 1977), p. 136.

25. Don Ihde, *Consequences of Phenomenology* (Albany: State University of New York Press, 1986), pp. 72-73.

26. Stephen W. Laycock and James G. Hart, eds., *Essays in Phenomenological Theology* (Albany: State University of New York Press, 1986), p. 8.

27. Paul S. Johnson, *Psychology of Religion* (New York: Abingdon Press, 1959), p. 276.

28. Walter T. Ong, *Orality and Literacy: The Technologizing of the Word* (New York: Routledge, 1988), p. 74.

29. Ong, *The Presence of the Word*, p. 119.

30. Ong, *The Presence of the Word*, p. 309.

31. Victor Turner, *The Ritual Process: Structure and Anti-Structure* (Ithaca, NY: Cornell University Press, 1977), pp. 169, 237.

32. Victor Turner, *Dramas, Fields and Metaphors: Symbolic Action in Human Society* (Ithaca, NY: Cornell University Press, 1974), p. 237.

33. Turner, *The Ritual Process*, p. 96.

34. John Lovell, Jr., *Black Song: The Forge and the Flame, The Story of How the Afro-American Spiritual Was Hammered Out* (New York: Macmillan, 1972), p. 521.

35. Rudolph Otto, *The Idea of the Holy* (New York: Oxford University Press, 1924), p. 13.

36. McLuhan, *The Gutenberg Galaxy*, p. 22.

37. McLuhan, *The Gutenberg Galaxy*, p. 25.

38. Ong, *The Presence of the Word*, p. 129.

39. Ong, *The Presence of the Word*, p. 130.

40. Ernst Cassirer, *Language and Myth* (New York: Dow Publications, 1969).

41. Robert Plant Armstrong, *The Powers of Presence: Conscious, Myth and Affective Presence* (Philadelphia: University of Pennsylvania Press, 1981); Robert Plant Armstrong, *The Affecting Presence: An Essay in Humanistic Anthropology* (Urbana: University of Illinois Press, 1971).

42. Robert Plant Armstrong, *The Affecting Presence: An Essay in Humanistic Anthropology*, pp. 43-44.

43. Ibid., pp. 48, 52.

44. See Melville J. Herskovits, *The Myth of the Negro Past* (New York: Alfred A. Knopf, 1941), p. 215; George E. Simpson, *Religious Cults of the Caribbean: Trinidad, Jamaica and Haiti* (Rio Piedras, Puerto Rico: University of Puerto Rico Press, 1970), p. 131; Walter Pitt, "Keep the Fire Burnin': Language and Ritual in the Afro-Baptist Church," *Journal of the American Academy of Religion* 56, no. 1 (1988): p. 82; Walter Mischel and Francis Mischel, "Psychological Aspects of Spirit Possession," *American Anthropologist* 60 (1958): 249.

45. Laycock and Hart, *Essays*, pp. 16-17.

46. Aidan Kavanagh, *On Liturgical Theology* (New York: Pueblo Publishing, 1984), p. 73.

47. Kavanagh, *On Liturgical Theology*, p. 75.

48. James H. Cone, *Black Theology and Black Power* (New York: Seabury Press, 1969); Gayraud S. Wilmore, *Black Religion and Black Radicalism* (Garden City, NY: Anchor Press, Doubleday, 1973).

49. E. Quita Craig, *Black Dance of the Federal Theatre Era* (Amherst: University of Massachusetts Press, 1980), p. 23.

50. Walter T. Ong, "World as View and World as Event," *American Anthropologist* 71 (August 1969): 63.

Bibliography

Armstrong, Robert Plant. *The Affecting Presence: An Essay In Humanistic Anthropology.* Urbana: University of Illinois Press, 1971.

———. *The Powers of Presence: Conscious, Myth and Affective Presence.* Philadelphia: University of Pennsylvania Press, 1981.

Cassirer, Ernst. *Language and Myth.* New York: Dow Publications, 1969.

Cone, James H. *Black Theology and Black Power.* New York: Seabury Press, 1969.

———. "Black Theology and Black Women," introductory essay in *Black Theology: A Documentary History, 1966-1979.* Edited by Gayraud S. Wilmore and James H. Cone. Maryknoll, NY: Orbis Books, 1979.

Craig, E. Quita. *Black Dance of the Federal Theatre Era.* Amherst: University of Massachusetts Press, 1980.

Doty, William G. *Mythography: The Study of Myths and Rituals.* Tuscaloosa: University of Alabama Press, 1991.

Goody, Jack. *The Interface Between the Written and the Oral.* Cambridge: Cambridge University Press, 1987.

———. *The Logic of Writing and the Organization of Society.* Cambridge: Cambridge University Press, 1986.

Goody, Jack and Ian Watt. "The Consequences of Literacy." *Comparative Studies in Society and History* 5, no. 3 (1963): 306.

Grimes, Ronald L. *Beginnings of Ritual Studies*. Washington, DC: University Press of America, 1982.

Hart, Kevin. *The Trespass of the Sign*. Cambridge: Cambridge University Press, 1991.

Havelock, Eric A. *The Literate Revolution in Greece and Its Cultural Consequences*. Princeton, NJ: Princeton University Press, 1982.

Herskovits, Melville J. *The Myth of the Negro Past*. New York: Alfred A. Knopf, 1941.

Ihde, Don. *Listening and Voice: A Phenomenology of Sound*. Athens: Ohio University Press, 1976.

——. *Consequences of Phenomenology*. Albany: State University of New York Press, 1986.

Johnson, Paul S. *Psychology of Religion*. New York: Abingdon Press, 1959.

Kavanagh, Aidan. *On Liturgical Theology*. New York: Pueblo Publishing, 1984.

Laycock, Stephen W. and James G. Hart, eds. *Essays in Phenomenological Theology*. Albany: State University of New York Press, 1986.

Lovell, Jr., John. *Black Song: The Forge and the Flame: The Story of How the Afro-American Spiritual Was Hammered Out*. New York: Macmillan, 1972.

Mischel, Walter and Francis Mischel. "Psychological Aspects of Spirit Possession." *American Anthropologist* 60 (1958).

Mueller-Vollmer, Kurt. *The Hermeneutics Reader: Texts of the German Tradition from the Enlightenment to the Present*. New York: Continuum, 1989.

Ong, Walter T. *Interfaces of the World: Studies in the Evolution of Consciousness and Culture*. Ithaca, NY: Cornell University Press, 1977.

——. *Orality and Literacy: The Technologizing of the Word*. New York: Routledge, 1988.

——. *The Presence of the Word*. Minneapolis: University of Minnesota Press, 1967.

——. "World as View and World as Event." *American Anthropologist* 71 (August 1969): 63.

Otto, Rudolf. *The Idea of the Holy: An Inquiry into the Non-Rational Factor in the Idea of the Divine and its Relation to the Rational.* London: Oxford University Press, 1924.

Pitt, Walter. "Keep the Fire Burnin': Language and Ritual in the Afro-Baptist Church." *Journal of the American Academy of Religion* 56, no. 1 (1988): 78, 82. This article also appears in *American Ethnologist* 16 (May 1989).

Raboteau, Albert J. *Slave Religion.* New York: Oxford University Press, 1980.

Simpson, George E. *Religious Cults of the Caribbean: Trinidad, Jamaica and Haiti.* Rio Piedras, Puerto Rico: University of Puerto Rico Press, 1970.

Spiegelberg, Herbert. *Doing Phenomenology: Essays on and In Phenomenology* The Hague: Martinus Nijhoff, 1975.

Turner, Victor. *Dramas, Fields and Metaphors: Symbolic Action in Human Society.* Ithaca, NY: Cornell University Press, 1974.

——. *The Ritual Process: Structure and Anti-Structure.* Ithaca, NY: Cornell University Press, 1977.

Tillich, Paul. *Systematic Theology.* Vol. I. Chicago: University of Chicago Press, 1983.

Williams, Melvin D. *Community in a Black Pentecostal Church: An Anthropological Study.* Prospect Heights, IL: Waveland Press, 1984.

Wilmore, Gayraud S. *Black Religion and Black Radicalism.* Garden City, NY: Anchor Press, Doubleday, 1973.

Index